Mother and Son, Lisdoonvarna (Lawrence Collection National Library of Ireland)

ART BYRNE & SEAN McMAHON

FACES OF THE WEST

1875   1925

A Record of Life in the West of Ireland

Photographic   Literary

Dedicated to our wives

First published 1976 by
The Appletree Press Limited
6 Dublin Road, Belfast BT2 7HL

Designed by
Spring Graphics Co.

Printed by
The Appletree Press Ltd.
4 Marcus Ward Street, Belfast BT7 1AP

Cloth ISBN 0 904651 12 6
Paper ISBN 0 904651 11 8

c.1976, Appletree Press Ltd.

Contents

Preface

OUR THANKS ARE DUE to the National Library of Ireland; the staff of the Library of the Institute of Continuing Education (NUU), Magee College, Derry, especially Alan Roberts; the staff of the Belfast Central Library; Peter Folan of the Library of UCG; Nora Niland and Hubert Geelan of the Sligo County Library and Museum; Desmond Wynne of Castlebar; Mother M. Enda, Sr Teresa Margaret, Seamus Sherry and John Heneghan of Foxford; Ronnie O'Gorman, Tom Kenny, Maurice Semple of Galway: the Lynches of Lisdoovarna; Declan Bree, Eileen Lambert of Sligo; Rev Martin Coen of Craughwell; Annie Giblin of Castlerea; Rosaleen Conifrey of Leitrim Co Library; Kay O'Connor, Ballinrobe; Eileen Higgins and Eamon O'Boyle of Claremorris; Jackie Clarke of Ballina; Greagóir O Dughaill and Frank Corr of the State Paper Office, Dublin Castle; George Thompson and Nicholas Love of Manorhamilton; P. Keaney of Carrick-on-Shannon; James Finn and Miss Gavin of Roscommon; Liam Jordan of Ballinasloe, Brian Walker of Belfast and Jim Craig and Frank D'Arcy of Derry.

Introduction

FACES OF THE WEST is a record in picture and literary excerpt of life in the west of Ireland on both sides of the century's turn. It is hard, almost impossible, to imagine the quality of life then (or in any past era) and conventional histories however excellent cannot hope to give us this sense of past time. We may well ask if we can ever understand or truly imagine what people like ourselves felt in those days. The world of our great-grandfathers exists if at all in the already failing memories of our own grandparents (and it takes a considerable effort on our part to realise that they too were once young). Yet there is a way to reach in imagination towards some concept of the lives that people lived then.

At Black Head, Co Clare 1914 (Lynch Collection Lisdoonvarna)

Thanks to photography , the new toy, we have permanent images of the past, perhaps a little stiff, deliberately posed often, but certainly in some way authentic. And if we add to these pictorial images other images from the imaginative writings of the time we can arrive at an acceptable version which will be true for us and not too false of them.

7

Our compilation is unashamedly a companion volume to Brian Mercer Walker's excellent *Faces of the Past*. It tries to do for the west of the country — mostly but not precisely the province of Connacht — what his book did so signally for Ulster. Unlike the northern province our area had no city, no urban literary tradition and no theatre. The occasional writings, sketches, lampoons, one-act plays that the period provided in abundance in Belfast and the stout northern towns were simply not there but by the law of unreasonable compensation the west provided most of the giants of the Irish literary revival. Lady Gregory, Edward Martyn, George Moore and of course, Yeats and Synge all had the strongest of connections with Connacht.

It was a region in which heavy industry, proletarian urban life and sociological anomie played little part in the life of people; there were peasants, small shopkeepers, half-mounted gentry and a rapidly increasing number of tourists. Our period, 1875 to 1925, was one of considerable change, socially and politically but it seemed to have a more muted effect upon the west than other places. What did produce by western standards a revolutionary change was the Plan of Campaign — the Land League's answer to Castle Rackrent. And it did have its meteors: the names of Michael Davitt and Captain Boycott are part of Connacht mythology, and so is that of Constance Markiewicz. The feeling of life, the sense of space, loneliness, hard work and distances painfully travelled is captured best in the literature of the time.

Tourist Boat on the River Shannon (Lawrence Collection, National Library of Ireland)

The photographs, in their formal way, show with equal effect the contrast between peasant cabin and Big House - the wildness and beauty of the terrain setting off the greatness of the houses, the opulence of the better hotels, and on the permanent way the elaboration of stonework and steel.

While we cannot question the deliberate artistry of the writer we might wonder if the photographer saw himself as more than a journeyman. Certainly in the one excerpt that we could find where a photographer is mentioned he is portrayed with less than respect. It is most likely that our two chief photographers were too concerned to get on with their jobs to worry unduly about their art, if indeed they considered it at all. The round of events: christenings, weddings, sports days, staff outings, visits by Personages filled their days. A Boycott Expedition or a Land League riot was an event rarely captured except by happy accident. As their work shows they were fine photographers but they would have been startled had anyone suggested that they were creative artists.

Robert French, the chief photographer who took the pictures for the Dublin firm of Lawrence, was born in Dublin in 1841 and after an early career which included service in the RIC, began to take photographs around 1880. Thomas J Wynne, a contemporary and friend of French (they frequently exchanged albums), is thought by his grandson, Desmond Wynne of Castlebar to have been born in America in 1838 but he afterwards settled in Castlebar. His collection is a fascinating record of life in Mayo in our period, with portfolios on the Lucan family, the Boycott affair, evictions, politics, amateur theatre and the events of life in a self-contained part of the country. He died in 1900 but not before he had established through his sons, branches in Loughrea, Tipperary and Portarlington. One further notable collection, that of Thady Kilgannon of Sligo perished in the town dump in 1951 — a fate which seems to have overtaken several other collections. Kilgannon logically enough extended his interest to moving pictures and became the proprietor of Sligo's two cinemas.

Our two viewpoints, those of writer and photographer, are necessarily different, and not just because of their different media. Often, surprisingly it is the photographer who gives the more romantic picture. Compare, for example, Jane Barlow's realistic description of peasant life with French's version of the girl and the donkey, which with Hinde-sight might be found on any modern revolving card-stand. His Galway women, too, seem too serene to engage in the fish-wife vituperation recorded by Somerville and Ross in *The Real Charlotte*. We can grasp little of the misery of Seumas O'Kelly's turf-seller in French's

9

study of the sturdy farmer with his load of turf in Ballinrobe. Then, of course, most of French's photographs are the perfect complement to Guinan's description. In the case of Lissadell House the photographer was more accurate than the poet: Yeat's 'great windows open to the south', maybe, but to the cold eye of the camera the place seems lumpish and illproportioned. One outstanding writer, perhaps in his optimistic

Lissadill House, Sligo (Lawrence Collection, National Library of Ireland)

way the most representative of the time, was Percy French who best came to terms for all his genial mocking, with the artifacts of the New Age. His songs of aeroplanes, motor-cars, bicycles were as commercially successful as the photographs. In general we have matched picture and text. The connection may not always be obvious but it does exist. We are responsible for selection but we hope that photograph and excerpt combined give an acceptable and not entirely subjective account of the west of Ireland of fifty to a hundred years ago.

Art Byrne & Sean McMahon

Ar Muir is ar Tír

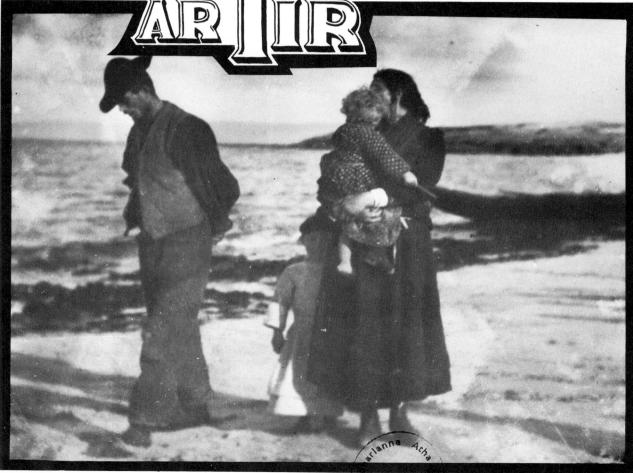

On Inisheer (Synge Collection, Trinity College)

The Pier, Inishmore, Aran (Lawrence Collection, National Library of Ireland).

"FRIENDS," BEGAN O'MALLEY in Irish, addressing his peasant followers. "I am glad to have an opportunity to speak here to-day to these gentlemen who have come from the mainland. I am going to address these gentlemen in English since they do not understand their own native language, but I ask you as the descendants of the ancient clansmen of the O'Malleys to see that I get a hearing. If anybody wants to create a disturbance in order to prevent me from saying what I have to say, let us see to it that he will get the worst of the argument. We ruled this island for centuries before the foreigner came with their yardsticks and their beer measures to rob us of our birthright, but we are not conquered yet and we will to-day make that clear to them."

There were loud cries of "O'Mailleach Abu" and waving of blackthorn sticks, and then O'Malley turned to the important people on the platform and, clearing his throat, spoke in English.

"I am speaking now to you priests and politicians, and the deluded people who follow you. You have come here to-day to hold a meeting, to try and foist your Home Rule programme on the natives of Inverara. As an O'Malley and the descendant of the chiefs who ruled over this island, I came to utter a protest. You priests and you politicians are the curse of this country" (here there were cries of protest, but the cries of protest were drowned in shouts of "Mailleach Abu," and Fr. O'Reilly raised his hand for silence, although the pimple on his nose was swelling and appeared to be on the point of bursting). "Ireland needs to be rid of her 'Gentry', to be rid of those descendants of adventurers, who were picked by marauding English generals from the London brothels and foisted on this country as 'gentlemen'. Ireland needs to be rid of those dissolute, roystering, ignorant scoundrels, who have never done anything for the country but rob it, except when once and again the dung of their stables has been raked by the hand of fate and they have produced a Moore or a Parnell.

"And after them, Ireland wants to be rid of her priests and politicians" (renewed cries of protest, which threatened this time to end in blows, but the parish priest again came to the rescue, even though he himself was trembling with wrath, and Fr. Considine's face was hidden behind his red silk handkerchief to hide his anger). "Ireland needs to be rid of her priests and politicians, for they are the two main forces that are keeping the country in ignorance. When she is free of these three scourges she can advance.

"And I want to point out," he continued, raising his voice, "that this objective cannot be gained by begging from British Kings, or by prayer to God, or by speeches. It can only be gained by the same methods by which the Land League men won the land, by reliance on our own brawn and muscle, and by our willingness to die for the mother that gave us all birth" (here there was a cheer even from the natives of Kilmurrage, and the young man in the grey tweed suit and the straw hat, who was now standing beside Cissy Carmody, waved his hat in the air and shouted "To hell with the King").

Liam O'Flaherty, *Thy Neighbour's Wife*, (London, 1923) pp73-75.

LIAM O'FLAHERTY was born on Inishmore, Aran in 1897. After a spell at a seminary in Dublin he left to become an undergraduate at UCD. When the war started he joined the Irish Guards and was shell-shocked and invalided out. His experiences in the war provided the background for one of his lesser known but effective novels. *The Return of the Brute* (1929). His active period as a socialist revolutionary was short but he has remained true to the socialist ideal. Popularly known as the author of *The Informer* (1925), his fame will rest on his short stories both in English and in Irish. *Duil* (1953) contained the best of his writing in Irish. His autobiography, *Shame The Devil* (1934) deserves reprinting.

'. . . so I sat down on the slip and drew out my wallet of photographs. In an instant I had the whole band clambering round me, in their ordinary mood.'

J M Synge, *The Aran Islands*, (Dublin, 1907)

Synge left his photographs and camera to his nephew, Edward M. Stephens, and they were eventually published with his wife, Lilo's permission in 1971. The camera was a Klito, a plate-changing model made by Haughton's of London.

A currach by the pier at Inishmaan [Synge Collection, Trinity College].

THE grand road from the mountain goes shining to the sea,
    And there is traffic in it and many a horse and cart,
But the little roads of Cloonagh are dearer far to me,
    And the little roads of Cloonagh go rambling through my heart.

A great storm from the ocen goes shouting o'er the hill,
    And there is a glory in it and terror on the wind,
But the haunted air of twilight is very strange and still,
    And the little winds of twilight are dearer to my mind.

The great waves of the Atlantic sweep storming on the way,
    Shining green and silver with the hidden herring shoal,
But the Little Waves of Breffny have drenched my heart in spray,
    And the Little Waves of Breffny go stumbling through my soul.

Eva Gore-Booth, 'The Little Waves of Breffny', from *Selected Poems* (Dublin, undated)

EVA GORE-BOOTH was the younger sister of Constance Marciewicz and in her quiet way just as politically concerned as her more flamboyant sister. Born at Lissadell in 1870 her poetry was quasi-philosophical and mystical. '*The Little Waves of Breffny*' is a favourite anthology piece. She died in 1926.

ACHILL, much the largest of the off-shore islands, became a tourist centre in the eighteen-nineties with the building of an iron swivel-bridge. Till then its main source of revenue was fishing, which was profuse but unorganised, a fact which irritated many economically minded Victorian visitors. A Mr. J. G. V. Porter suggested it as the site for a 'magnificent imperial sea-fish aquarium; but, characteristically nothing came of it.

Achill People (Lawrence Collection, National Library of Ireland)

THE "ISLAND CHAPEL," as everyone called it, was an old-fashioned, cruciform building, wide, squat and low, unlovely in its architecture and furnished in the plainest and poorest style. It had two gloomy galleries, entered from the outside by means of big, ungainly stone stairs, whose rough-hewn steps were worn thin by the feet of generation after generation of devout worshippers. Everything, in a word, in and about the "Island Chapel" was antiquated, dim and faded, unmistakably proclaiming that it was a poor man's church. Not that it was not always clean and neat, for Susan Conrahy never allowed a speck of dust or rust to rest on anything. All the same, in spite of her oft repeated washing, scrubbing and scouring, she was unable to counteract the wear and tear of time. Indeed, the people somehow liked their old chapel all the better for its congenial poverty, and those of them who occasionally heard Mass in grander churches used to say that they felt much more at home in their own dear, dingy "Island Chapel," and could pray far better in it, as there was no grandeur there to distract their thoughts.

Although it was the principal parochial church, everyone spoke of it as the "Island Chapel." When Father Devoy came to the parish, he began to call it "the Island Church;" but he soon found he was constantly misunderstood, as that term was exclusively applied to the Protestant place of worship in the district, a dismal-looking structure, attended on Sunday afternoons by about a dozen people, or thereabouts. However, although he frequently protested against the popular misapplication of the term, "church", in this connection, he could not wean his people from calling their place of worship by the more homely and familiar name of "the chapel", and was, consequently, obliged to fall in with custom himself.

Joseph Guinan, *The Island Parish*, (Dublin, 1908) pp 115-116

THE REV. JOSEPH GUINAN, famous as the author of *The Soggarth Aroon* (1905), a title cribbed from John Banim. His accounts of life among the poor peasants of the West are based upon first-hand experience but are a little sentimental and emotional by to-day's standards.

Below: *Bannacurry Monastery, Achill (Lawrence Collection, National Library of Ireland*

THE YOUNG MAN has been buried, and his funeral was one of the strangest scenes I have met with. People could be seen going down to his house from early in the day, yet when I went there with the old man about the middle of the afternoon, the coffin was still lying in front of the door, with the men and women of the family standing round beating it, and keening over it, in a great crowd of people. A little later every one knelt down and a last prayer was said. Then the cousins of the dead man got ready two oars and some pieces of rope - the men of his own family seemed too broken with grief to know what they were doing - the coffin was tied up, and the procession began. The old women walked close behind the coffin, and I happened to take a place just after them, among the first of the men. The rough lane to the graveyard slopes away towards the east, and the crowd of women going down before me in their red dresses, cloaked with red petti-coats, with the waistband that is held round the head just seen from behind, had a strange effect, to which the white coffin and the unity of colour gave a nearly cloistral quietness.

This time the graveyard was filled with withered grass and bracken instead of the early ferns that were to be seen everywhere at the other funeral I have spoken of, and the grief of the people was of a different kind, as they had come to bury a young man who had died in his first manhood, instead of an old woman of eighty. For this reason the keen lost a part of its formal nature, and was recited as the expression of intense personal grief by the young men and women of the man's own family.

When the coffin had been laid down, near the grave that was to be opened, two long switches were cut from the brambles among the rocks, and the length and breadth of the coffin were marked on them. Then the men began their work, clearing off stones and thin layers of earth, and breaking up an old coffin that was in the place into which the new one had to be lowered. When a number of blackened boards and pieces of bone had been thrown up with the clay, a skull was lifted out, and placed upon a gravestone. Immediately the old woman, the mother of the dead man, took it up in her hands, and carried it away be herself. Then she sat down and put it in her lap - it was the skull of her own mother - and began keening and shrieking over it with the wildest lamentation.

As the pile of mouldering clay got higher beside the grave a heavy smell began to rise from it, and the men hurried with their work, measuring the hole repeat-edly with the two rods of bramble. When it was nearly deep enough the old woman got up and came back to the coffin, and began to beat on it, holding the skull in her left hand. This last moment of grief was the most terrible of all. The young women were nearly lying among the stones, worn out with their passion of grief, yet raising themselves every few moments to beat with magnificent gestures on the boards of the coffin. The young men were worn out also, and their voices cracked continually in the wail of the keen.

When everything was ready the sheet was unpinned from the coffin, and it was lowered into its place. Then an old man took a wooden vessel with holy water in it, and a wisp of bracken, and the people crowded round him while he splashed the water over them. They seemed eager to get as much of it as possible, more than one old woman crying out with a humor-ous voice - 'Tabhair dham braon eile, a Mhourteen.' ('Give me another drop, Martin.')

When the grave was half filled in, I wandered round towards the north watching two seals that were chasing each other near the surf. I reached the Sandy Head as the light began to fail, and found some of the men I knew best fishing there with a sort of drag-net. It is a tedious process, and I sat for a long time on the sand watching the net being put out, and then drawn in again by eight men working together with a slow rhythmical movement.

As they talked to me and gave me a little poteen and a little bread when they thought I was hungry, I could not help feeling that I was talking with men who were under a judgement of death. I knew that every one of them would be drowned in the sea in a few years and battered naked on the rocks, or would die in his own cottage and be buried with another fearful scene in the graveyard I had come from.

J.M. SYNGE, *The Aran Islands*

ACHILL DISASTER: Twenty-three out of a hundred migrant workers were drowned when the hooker taking them from Daly's Point to Westport capsized. They were mostly in their teens and indeed for many it was their first trip to Scotland for the harvest. What seems to have happened was that in their excitement at seeing the Glasgow steamer for the first time they stood up and caused the boat to overturn. Many more would have been lost but for the action of the crew of the steamer. The bodies were brought as far as Mallaranny by train on the new line that was being built from Westport to Achill Sound.

SYNGE'S GENIUS as a dramatist has tended to obscure his talent as prose writer. It is probably true that he needed the time on Aran to organise his gifts, though the results were by no means as magical as Yeats might have boasted. Anyway the account of his Aran sojourns and of his wanderings in Wicklow, Kerry and Connemara is written in prose of the highest quality.

The Aftermath of the Achill Disaster, June 1894 (Wynne Collection, Castlebar)

Fish Curing at Clare Island [Lawrence Collection National Library of Ireland]

MY black flocks wander on the bitter salt marshes;
  In the mist they feed and drink:
They pick at the sea-holly and and rough plants and grasses
  At the harsh water's brink.

My white flocks stray about the landward meadows: Their fleeces shine;
With lowered heads they feed on the tender herbs and grasses
  Tasting their honey-wine.

But my horned sheep spring and go upon the mountains
  Lifting their heads to the wind;
Out on the crags they stand; they drink of the running water,
  In the way of their kind.

Grace Rhys, '*Wild Pastures from* (*A Celtic
Anthology*, London, 1927) p132.

Connemara Girls (Lawrence Collection, National Library of Ireland).

AT THE DUFFCLANE END a donkey may now and then be met carrying a tall pyramid of chocolate-brown turf-sods, based on two pendant panniers, between which his large head bobs patiently, while beneath the load his slender, tottering legs take quick staccato steps, each scarcely the length of one of his own ears; or an old woman comes by with a creel projecting quaintly under her dark-blue cloak; or a girl saunters barefooted after a single file of gabbling geese, knitting along grey stocking as she goes, and never seeming to lift her eyes from the twinkle of her needles. But after you have gone a short way the chances are that you will meet nothing more civilised and conversable than wild birds and very large gnats, until you come in sight of Lisconnel.

Just before that, the road starts abruptly, as if it had suddenly taken fright at its own loneliness, and dips down a steepish slope, but quickly pulls itself up, finding that escape is impossible. The hill, whose spur it has thus crossed, is very insignificant, only a knoll-like *knockawn*, prolonged on the left hand as a low ridge, soon dwindling into a mere bank, and imperceptibly ceasing from the face of the resurgent bog. Yet it probably fixed the site of Lisconnel, because it offered some protection from the full sweep of the west wind, and because its boulder-strewn slopes, and a narrow strip at their foot, have a covering of poor light soil in which potatoes can be set. Such advantages seldom recur within a radius of several miles. For when I spoke of the spaciousness of Lisconnel I did not mean that there is much room in it for you or me, or anybody who must needs have "a bit of lan" to live on. The craggy ridge is surmounted by a few weather-worn thorn bushes, and one ash tree, so strongly warped to the eastward that a glance at it on the stillest day creates an impression of blasts blowing roughly. Also, after the manner of trees thus situated, it

seems to draw down and diffuse the very spirit of the desolate surrounding solitudes. The cabins themselves look somehow as if they felt its spell, and were huddling together for company. Three in a row on one side of the road, a couple fast by on the other - not exactly facing them, because of a swampy patch - two more a few paces further on, with "Ody Rafferty's" and "the widow M'Gurk's", which stand "a trifle back o' the road" up the hillslopes, climbing down to join the group. That is all Lisconnel, unless we count in the O'Driscolls' old dwelling, whose roof has long since top-dressed a neighbouring field, and whose walls are in some places peered over by the nettles.

Cabin walls in Lisconnel are built of rough stones with no mortar, and not mud enough to preclude a great deal of unscientific ventilation, which, maybe, has its advantages, dearly paid for through many a shivering night. All its roofs are thatched, but none of them with straw, which is too scarce for such a use. Rushes serve instead, not quite satisfactorily, being neither so warm nor so durable, nor even so picturesque, for their pale grey-green looks crude and cold, and the weather only bleaches it into a more colourless drab, when straw would be mellowly golden and russet. A thick fringe of stones must hang along the eaves, or roof and rafters would part company the first time the wind got a fair undergrip of the thatch.

Jane Barlow, *Irish Idylls* (London, 1892) pp 5-7

JANE BARLOW was born in Clontarf in 1857, daughter of the Rev. James Barlow who became Vice-Provost of Trinity College Dublin. Though she wrote poems her prose writings are superior. *Irish Idylls* (1892) shows a remarkable understanding and appreciation of peasant life in the West where all of her work is set. She died in 1917.

(Séachaideann fear maide dhó, cuireann sé sop féir timchioll air;
tosaigheann se dh'á chasadh, agus Síghle ag tabhairt amach an fhéir dó.)

MAC UI h-ANN. (ag gabhail) -

Ta péarla mná 'tabhairt soluis dúinn,
Is í mos ghrádh, is í mo rún,
'Sí Úna bhán, an righ-bhean   chiuin,
'S ni thuigid na Muimhnigh leath a stuaim.

  Atá na Muimhnigh seo dallta ag Dia,
Ni aithnighid eala thar lacha liath,
Acht tiucfaidh sí liom-sa, mo Hélen bhreágh

McKeown's Industry, Leenane. (Lawrence Collection, National Library of Ireland).

Mar a molfar a pearsa 's a sgéimh go bráth.

Ara! mhuise! mhuise! Nach é seo an baile breágh lághach, nach é seo an baile thar bárr, an baile a mbíonn an oiread sin rógaire crochta ann nach mbíonn aon easbhuidh rópa ar na daoinibh, leis an méad rópa ghoideann siad ó'n gcrochaire. Cráidhteacháin atá ionnta. Tá na rópaidh aca agus ní thugann siad uatha iad - acht go gcuireann siad an Connachtach bocht ag casadh sugáin dóibh! Níor chas siad sugán féir in san mbaile seo ariamh - agus an méad sughán cnáibe ata aca de bhárr an chrochaire!

> Gnidheann Connachtach ciallmhar
> Rópa dhó féin,
> Acht goideann an Muimhneach
> Ó'n gcrochaire é!
> Go bhfeicidh mé rópa
> Breágh cnáibe go fóill
> D'á fhásgadh ar sgóigibh
> Gach aoinne ann so!

Mar gheall ar aon mhnaoi amháin d'imthigheadar na Gréagaigh, agus níor stopadar agus níor mhór-chómnuigheadar no gur sgriosadar an Traoi, agus mar gheall ar aon mhnaoi amháin béidh an baile seo damanta go deó na ndeór agus go bruinne an bhrátha, le Dia na ngrás, go síorruidhe suthain, nuair nár thuigeadar gur ab í Úna ní Ríogáin an dara Helen do rugadh in a measg, agus go rug sí bárr áille ar Helen agus ar Bhénus, ar a dtáinig riompi agus ar dtiucfas 'na diaigh.

> Acht tiucfaidh sí liom mo phéarla mná
> Go cúige Connacht na ndaoine breágh;
> Gheobhaidh sí féasta fíon a's feóil,
> Rinnceanna árda, spórt a's ceól.

O! mhuise! mhuise! nár éirighidh an ghrian ar an mbaile seo, agus nár lasaidh réalta air, agus nár -
Ta sé san am so amuigh thar an dorus. Eirigheann na fir uile agus dúnaid é d'aon ruaig amháin air. Tugann Úna léim chum an doruis, acht beirid na mná uirri. Téidheann Séamus anonn chuici.

Dubhglas De hÍde, ''Casadh an tSúgáin'' Samhain 1901. ltn. 28,29.

DOUGLAS HYDE, 'An Craoibhín Aoibhinn' was born on January 17, 1862, in Co. Roscommon but spent most of his youth and early manhood at Frenchpark int he same county where his father was minister. Educated at home he learned Irish locally, a fact which turned him from two likely careers in the Church and the Law. His paper, 'The Necessity for De-Anglicising Ireland' on November 25, 1892 was followed the next summer by the founding with Eoin MacNeill of the Gaelic League. His best known books are *The Love Songs of Connacht* (1893) and *Mise agus an Conradh* (1937). He became first president of the state whose culture he helped to form. He died in 1949.
Casadh an tSúgáin (*The Twisting of the Rope*) was based upon a West of Ireland folktale. It tells how a wandering Connacht poet drives to distraction the decent people of a Munster house by his greed, railing and boasting. Hospitality prevents them from ejecting him but one evening while the family are making straw ropes for thatching he demonstrates his skill and twists himself out of the house. The piece printed describes the final exorcism. It was the first play in modern Irish and was first performed on October 21, 1901 at the Gaiety Theatre, Dublin.

Ropemaking on Aran [Synge Collection, Trinity College]

In ropemaking, two men usually sat together, one of them hammering the straw with a heavy block of wood to make it more pliable, the other forming the untwisted rope. The actual twisting was done by a boy or girl with a bent stick. The boastfulness of the poet in Hyde's play is all the more contemptible since the work of twisting was inappropriate for a man.

TRANSPORT & TOURISM

SOMEWHERE about forty years ago, when old gentlemen had faint recollections of their grandfathers wearing swords, and fast young gentlemen sneered at the "old square-toes" for doing so; before steam had puffed out all recollection of those barbarous days, when a gentleman's honor was deemed of more value than his bond, and some few years before the laying down of the electric telegraph, or the raising up of 18,B, * on a fine evening in the month of August, 18—, the "Tallyho" day coach, running between Dublin and L——, was seen passing through the principal entrance of Dalystown, a fine old place, situate and being, (as my friends of the legal profession would say,) in the county of Galway, and bordering the counties of Mayo and Roscommon.

This invasion of private property, on the part of the Tallyho, was accounted for by the coachman, who informed one of his passengers that by getting in at this gate, driving right through the demesne, and coming out on the opposite side, they avoided the half circle which the public road made, and shortened the distance fully a mile.

It was much pleasanter too, to bowl along the smooth gravelled avenue, than to travel the hilly, rutty road. So he was very glad to avail himself of the privilege of passing through the demesne, kindly given to him by the owner.

As the coach came in view of the house, and elderly gentleman and a young girl were seen standing at the hall door, anxiously watching its approach, while a number of domestics and laborers were grouped around the entrance to the stables and farm yard, evincing, by their eager looks, that the approach of the Tallyho was watched, on this evening, with unusual interest.

Suddenly a man, dressed in an old, faded hunting coat, tattered corduroys, his feet and legs free from the innovations of shoes and stockings, jumped up from the grass on which he had been lying, and as the coach came within a few yards of him, he cast a keen look up at its roof, then flinging an old hunting cap high in the air, he shouted, as he headed the coach, "Yoicks, Tallyho! here he comes, master, Mr. Henry himself, there's his handsome face, behind Joe. Yoicks, Tallyho".

Dillon O'Brien, *The Dalys of Dalystown* (St Paul, 1866) pp 10,11

32 *Salthill, Galway [Lawrence Collection, The National Library of Ireland]*

DILLON O'BRIEN was born at Kilmore, Co. Roscommon in 1817 and became Government teacher at the Indian Mission at La Pointe, Minnesota. He later settled in St. Paul and began to write what are literally Irish-American novels since the action takes place in both countries. As one who did well in the States he tends to use them as the source of *Di ex Machinis* to resolve the problems of his Irish characters. *The Dalys of Dalystown* (1866) is his best known novel and here typically money earned in America enables the hero, young Daly, to buy back the family estates and resume benevolent landlordism.

"We left Galway for Clifden at 9.30 next morning. The public conveyance is a large-paper edition of the outside car, with an elevated seat for the driver. There is one place to be avoided on some of these vehicles, that nearest to the horses on the offside, on account of the iron bar of the drag, which operates from time to time very disagreeably on the back and shoulders of the contiguous traveller."

S Reynold Hole: *A Little Tour of Ireland* (London 1896)

The Galway and Salthill Tramway was constructed in 1879. It was horsedrawn and ran from Eyre Square through the city and out to Salthill. Labour troubles and the war killed the company and petrol buses came in 1919.

The station in Galway was built in 1851 at the height of the great railway expansion. The line from Westport to Achill Sound built in the mid-1890's was really the twilight of this enterprise. The photograph shows the building of a traditional stone-bridge, which is rather unusual since by then most railway bridges were being built of iron.

Railway Station, Galway [Lawrence Collection, The National Library of Ireland]

Right: *Building the railway bridge at Newport in the eighteen-nineties (Wynne Collection, Castlebar)*

IT WAS THE EVE of the Parnell celebration in Dublin, and the town was full of excursionists waiting for a train which was to start at midnight. When Michael left me I spent some time in an hotel, and then wandered down to the railway.

A wild crowd was on the platform, surging round the train in every stage of intoxication. It gave me a better instance than I had yet seen of the half-savage temperament of Connaught. The tension of human excitement seemed greater in this insignificant crowd than anything I have felt among enormous mobs in Rome or Paris.

There were a few people from the islands on the platform, and I got in along with them to a third-class carriage. One of the women of the party had her niece with her, a young girl from Connaught who was put beside me; at the other end of the carriage there were some old men who were talking in Irish, and a young man who had been a sailor.

When the train started there were wild cheers and cries on the platform, and in the train itself the noise was intense; men and women shrieking and singing and beating their sticks on the partitions. At several stations there was a rush to the bar, so the excitement increased as we proceeded.

At Ballinasloe there were some soldiers on the platform looking for places. The sailor in our compartment had a dispute with one of them, and in an instant the door was flung open and the compartment was filled with reeling uniforms and sticks. Peace was made after a moment of uproar and the soldiers got out, but as they did so a pack of their women followers thrust their bare heads and arms into the doorway, cursing and blaspheming with extraordinary rage.

As the train moved away a moment later, these women set up a frantic lamentation. I looked out and caught a glimpse of the wildest heads and figures I have ever seen, shrieking and screaming and waving their naked arms in the light of the lanterns.

As the night went on girls began crying out in the carriage next to us, and I could hear the words of obscene songs when the train stopped at a station.

In our own compartment the sailor would allow no one to sleep, and talked all night with sometimes a touch of wit or brutality, and always with a wonderful fluency with wild temperament behind it.

The old men in the corner, dressed in black coats that had something of the antiquity of heirlooms, talked all night among themselves in Gaelic. The young girl beside me lost her shyness after a while, and let me point out the features of the country that were beginning to appear through the dawn as we drew near Dublin. She was delighted with the shadows of the trees - trees are rare in Connaught - and with the canal, which was beginning to reflect the morning light. Every time I showed her some new shadow she cried out with naïve excitement -

'Oh, it's lovely, but I can't see it.'

This presence at my side contrasted curiously with the brutality that shook the barrier behind us. The whole spirit of the west of Ireland, with its strange wildness and reserve, seemed moving in this single train to pay a last homage to the dead statesman of the east.

J. M. SYNGE *The Aran Islands*
(Dublin, 1907)

"WHERE TO NOW"

"WHERE TO NOW, your Excellency?" he inquired, dismally enough.

"To bl—zes!" answered his Excellency.

It was the first time the smooth, smiling lips of Lord Carlisle had shaped a profane syllable. Before decorum could stop the words they were out. But decorum resumed command the next instant.

"Ay, to blazes, to be sure," he continued, in quite an altered tone of voice, with a look of mild reproach at the tittering *aide-de-camp*. "But what blazes? that is the question. The blazing fire that this morning browned our toast in the best parlor of Mack's Hotel in Galway, or the blazes that are perhaps kindly cooking our dinners in Cong? Any blazes, or, at least, almost any blazes, were welcome on such an evening as this." He gazed as he spoke, with a half shudder, at the rain-blotted landscape, and smiled a sickly smile at his own sickly pleasantries.

"Cong is the nearest refuge — perhaps, I should rather say Galway is the farther of the two, your Excellency," interposed the private secretary.

"Then to Cong let it be," said Lord Carlisle, leaning back in his carriage, with a look of patient resignation.

Unlike the hotel from which they parted a good three hours ago, at Maam, the house is ablaze with light, and redolent with savoury odors. Now and again, from inside, a burst of jolly laughter drowns the fretful whining of the wind.

The very look of the place seemed to bid a cordial welcome to the wet, weary, and hungry travelers. A smile began to dawn on the pale face of this Excellency, as eyes, ears, nostrils gave him promise of a pleasant fare and comfortable quarters. The flickering smile disappeared in black despair when the host, whom a thundering peal upon the knocker brought to the door, spoke almost the same words as the churl of Maam, "No room for you here."

The Lord Carlisle's dignity yielded to his despair "I am the Lord Lieutenant!" he cried from his carriage.

"I could not let you in if you were the King," retorted the other. "Not even if you were the Pope of Rome, could you get in without leave.

"Who says a word against my good friend, his Holiness?" cried a rich jovial voice behind them, and the host drew aside respectfully, as a tall, burly figure, with a big face, as full of good humour as the sun is of light at midday, came striding down the passage and met the Viceroy face to face at the door.

"Big Joe!" cried Lord Carlisle in delighted amazement.

"Your Excellency," responded the other, with old-fashioned courtesy, "now and always at your service."

"Never needed it more, Joe," responded Lord Carlisle pitifully. I'd give my Garter for a dinner and bed. I have been turned like a beggarman out of all the hotels in Connemara."

"I'm afraid you will find it hard to get in here," said Big Joe, "You see, you are not the kind of guest that was expected, and I don't think you would like the company any more than they'd like you."

"Any company is good enough for me," said the other entreatingly, "if Big Joe M'Donnell is amongst them. But a good dinner would make the worst company in the world pleasant to me now."

Big Joe was silent for a moment. "I'll tell you the whole truth," he said, "and nothing but the truth. We hold our Patrick's day dinner here to-night. Every man is bound to tell a story or drink a quart of salt water; so there will be a good many stories," he added, with humorous twinkles in his eyes, "and they might not all suit the ears of his Excellency."

"His Excellency's ears are neither as long nor as tender as a donkey's" was the curt reply, "and his Excellency's teeth are as hungry as a wolf's."

"Well, if they don't mind hearing they might mind telling," said Joe. "There is very little Castle company amongst us to-night, and some of the yarns spun might be twisted into a hemp cravat for the neck of the spinner."

Lord Carlisle drew himself up haughtily, with an indignant flush upon his handsom old face. "I have sat at your table," he said, "and you have sat at mine. I did not expect that insinuation from Joe M'Donnell. There is some honor yet left even amongst Irish Lord Lieutenants."

Mathias McDonnell Bodkin *The Lord Lieutenant's Adventure*.

MATHIAS McDONNELL BODKIN was born in Tuam in 1849. He was Nationalist MP for North Roscommon and later a County Court Judge in Clare. His experiences as a judge provided him with much of his humorous material. He wrote plays under the pseudonym 'Crom a boo'. *The Lord Lieutenant's Adventure* is in its wildness and farcicality straight out of the Somerville and Ross stable, however much the Nationalist author might have wished to disclaim it.

THE RAILWAY HOTELS followed the building of the stations and were developed both for commercial reasons and for the ever-growing tourist trade. When the Galway-Clifden line was opened in 1895 the company organised a two-way omnibus service between Clifden and Westport so that these same tourists might do the wilds of Connemara in style and reasonable comfort. A 'Tourist Train' which took passengers from Dublin direct to Clifden ran from 1903 to 1906.

WHO were the builders? Question not the silence
That settles on the lake for evermore,
Save when the sea-bird screams and to the islands
The echo answers from the steep-cliffed shore.

O half-remaining ruin, in the lore
Of human life a gap shall all deplore
Beholding thee; since thou art like the dead
Found slain, no token to reveal the why,
The name, the story. Some one murder'd

We know, we guess, and gazing upon thee,
And, filled by the long silence of reply,
We guess some garnered sheaf of tragedy;—
Of tribe or nation slain so utterly

That even their ghosts are dead, and on their grave
Springeth no bloom of legend in its wilderness;
And age by age weak washing round the islands
No faintest sigh of story lisps the wave.

William Larminie, The Nameless Ruin, in *The Dublin
Book of Irish Verse* (Dublin 1909) pp. 498-9

WILLIAM LARMINIE was born in Castlebar in 1850. Unlike his Irish Renaissance colleagues, John Todhunter, Katherine Tynan and T W Rolleston, he preferred epic narrative poems to lyrics. He lived in England, working as a civil servant till an early retirement due to ill-health in 1888. Two years later he produced *Glanlua and Other Poems*. He was strongly influenced by heroic Irish themes and Gaelic prosody and his comparatively early death at Bray in 1900 may well have removed Yeat's one poetic rival.

Left: *Pigeon Hole, Cong. (Lawrence Collection, National Library of Ireland)*

"Lough Mask which is thirty-six feet higher than Lough Corrib, sends its surplus waters to the latter through one of those subterraneous channels common to the limestone formation, untill close to Cong, where the river rises, and soon after turns a corn mill. The stream is visible in several places on the passage; but the most remarkable opening is the Pigeon Hole, which is about a mile from Cong. The descent, about sixty feet, is not difficult; and by the assistance of a light the course of the stream can be traced in its caverned bed for a considerable distance. Taking the advantages of lake and mountain scenery which this place enjoys, together with its site, we cannot but regret that such a miserable village as Cong should occupy so important a position."
James Frazer: A Handbook for Travellers in Ireland (Dublin 1844)

THE CLADDAGH was an old fishing village on the far bank of the Corrib from Galway City. Its inhabitants had the sole right to fish in Galway Bay, hence its mention in the song Galway Bay. Originally the native Irish without the walls of the Norman city, they developed a rich tradition of separate life. The most famous relic of this tradition is the Claddagh Ring, consisting of two hands clasping a crowned heart, which has at present a certain chic as a wedding ring. Fishing was the prime-feature of life: the Dominican fathers established a 'piscatorial school' as early as 1846. All the nineteenth-century guide books are eloquent about the colour and life of the community. In 1934 it was demolished and replaced by modern houses. The word claddagh in Irish means 'sea-shore'.

Below and right: *The Claddagh, Galway* (*Lawrence Collection, National Library of Ireland*)

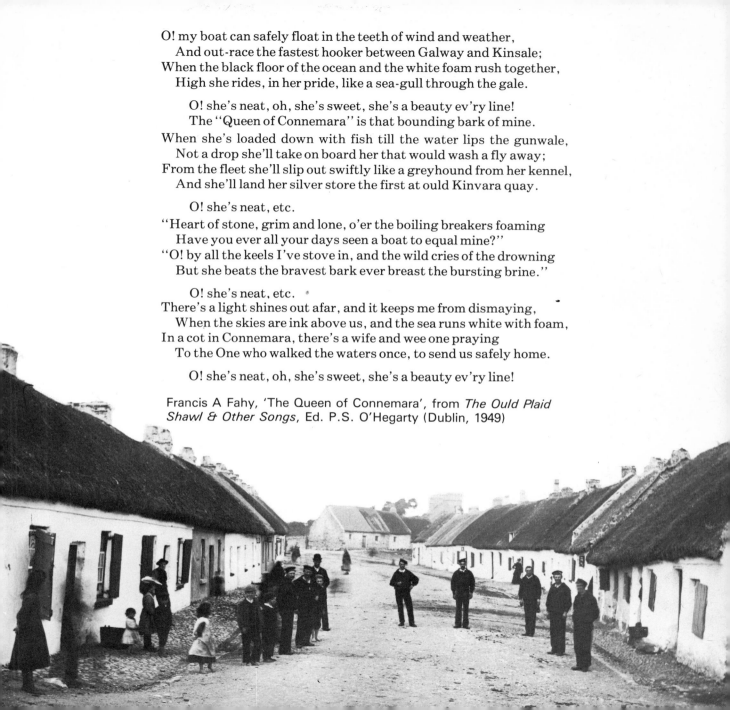

O! my boat can safely float in the teeth of wind and weather,
   And out-race the fastest hooker between Galway and Kinsale;
When the black floor of the ocean and the white foam rush together,
   High she rides, in her pride, like a sea-gull through the gale.

     O! she's neat, oh, she's sweet, she's a beauty ev'ry line!
     The "Queen of Connemara" is that bounding bark of mine.
When she's loaded down with fish till the water lips the gunwale,
   Not a drop she'll take on board her that would wash a fly away;
From the fleet she'll slip out swiftly like a greyhound from her kennel,
   And she'll land her silver store the first at ould Kinvara quay.

     O! she's neat, etc.
"Heart of stone, grim and lone, o'er the boiling breakers foaming
   Have you ever all your days seen a boat to equal mine?"
"O! by all the keels I've stove in, and the wild cries of the drowning
   But she beats the bravest bark ever breast the bursting brine."

     O! she's neat, etc.
There's a light shines out afar, and it keeps me from dismaying,
   When the skies are ink above us, and the sea runs white with foam,
In a cot in Connemara, there's a wife and wee one praying
   To the One who walked the waters once, to send us safely home.

     O! she's neat, oh, she's sweet, she's a beauty ev'ry line!

Francis A Fahy, 'The Queen of Connemara', from *The Ould Plaid Shawl & Other Songs*, Ed. P.S. O'Hegarty (Dublin, 1949)

Piers and Cliff, Enniscrone, Co. Sligo
(*Lawrence Collection, National Library of Ireland*)

Typical of the comic writing of the period, this was reprinted (from *The Jarvey*) because of its local interest, in the Sligo Independent of August 17, 1889. It is almost certainly by Percy French.

WILL WAGTAIL'S ACCOUNT OF HIS VISIT TO MULLAGHMORE

This pleasant little watering place, like many other another more pretentious seaside resort, is situated on the margin of the treacherous ocean.

The "loan of a fill of tobacco" to an old coastguardsman, elicited the information that it was the Atlantic ocean, and "there was no land nearther nor America."

A vehicle called "the long car" brings you and your luggage (if you have any) to Mullaghmore, but be careful not to say to any of the obsequious natives "Carry my luggage to the best hotel, my good man," as there is no hotel, and the remark shows you to be a stranger and a tourist.

The head landlord, the Hon. Evelyn Ashley, might convert his "palatial home" (good phrase) into "The Evelyn Arms," and drive a good business. An advertisement in *The Jarvey* and *Irish Cyclist* would be a wise beginning, but the scheme should be undertaken in a spirit of enterprise and industry to ensure success.

I forgot the name of the shop which provides Mullaghmore with the necessaries of life, but as there is only one emporium at present you are bound to patronise it.

There is not the slightest use bringing any illness or disease to this backward locality, as there is no doctor to tell you what to do under the circumstances.

As a natural consequence, there are no deaths, though births and marriages are recognised institutions.

I was so surprised to hear this (from the oldest inhabitant, too), that I went and interviewed the sexton. He assured me it was quite true, and that he himself was a mere amateur, and had never performed in public.

There is a very good sea fishing to be had, and the prices charged by the local dealers would fill the gay deceivers of Baggot Street or William Street with horror and despair, but not, I fear, with remorse.

The bathing is good, but the accommodation isn't, at least for ladies, as there are only a few bathing-boxes scattered along the coast.

For men, a well-aired roof is considered sufficient as a tiring chamber.

In my character of Official Lyre I thought it well to imbibe some poetical inspiration by watching some sea nymphs at their gambols in the "buoyant blue."

The lines underneath will show the hour was not a propitious one.

I insert here some spirited verses which I found carved in relief in a friend's note-book:

LINES ON MULLAGHMORE

Of all bewcheous situations
For tourists' recreations,
(I made these observations
   As I walk along the shore;)
The finest naval cinther
The Atlantic waves can inther,
In summer or in winther,
   Is lovely Mullaghmore.

And the valiant population,
They take their recreation
In pleasant conversation,
   Making bargains at the door;
Or maybe 'tis their pleasure,
In sport to pass their leisure,
For time has ne'er a measure
   At lovely Mullaghmore.

But I'm getting to dominions
Where the unambitious pinions
Of the Paygasus can niver
   Unaided hope to soar;
Och, while the rain's a-pourin',
And the ocean waves are roarin',
Who'd be thinkin' of Bundoran
   To compare with Mullaghmore.

LISDOONVARNA became known as Ireland's Premier Spa in the last quarter of the nineteenth-century. People flocked to take the waters from all over the country. The twin wells were of iron and magnesium and there was a sulphur well about a mile away. It early became a popular resort for the clergy where they felt themselves able to relax, as even a French traveller noticed:

"Je me rappelle, dans le vaste salon de l'hotel de l'Aigle, une quinzaine de ces révérends pères, — ainsi les appelle-t-on — buvant du punch au whisky et chantant à tour de rôle des chansons comiques bêtes à pleurer, et des romances sentimentales en facon de complainte d'aveugle."
Marie-Anne de Bovet, *Trois Mois en Irlande*(Paris, 1908)

FRANCIS ARTHUR FAHY was born in Kinvara, Co Galway in 1854. Famous for his song-lyrics which many thought were traditional (a fate he shared with Joseph Campbell and Padraic Colum), he lived in London from 1873 till his death in 1935. He was one of the founders of the London Branch of the Gaelic League and wrote books for children on Irish heritage including an *Irish History in Rhyme*. Though not so well known as some of his other pieces, such as 'Haste to the Wedding' and 'The Ould Plaid Shawl', 'The Bog Road, Lisdoonvarna' is typical of his work.

Twin Wells, Lisdoonvarna [Lawrence Collection, The National Library of Ireland]

THE BOG ROAD

Could I travel afar now
From Bantry to Barna,
'Tis to Lisdoonvarna
    My way I would find;
For there, one bright summer,
Myself, a new-comer,
Found mirth, fun, and humour
    That ne'er leaves my mind.
O! those who each season,
Without rhyme or reason,
Cross far foreign seas on
    To light the heart's load,
Know nought of the pleasure,
Without stint or measure,
That waits them with leisure
    Along the Bog Road.

'Tis there every morning,
Dull drowsiness scorning,
Stout lads without warning
    Roam over the hills,
While matron and widdy
(Lamenting "poor Biddy")
Take draughts that would rid ye,
    'Tis said, from all ills.
There farmers together
Discuss on the heather
The markets, the weather,
    The last crops they sowed;
While children are sporting,
Young couples resorting
Are cosily courting
    Along the Bog Road.

Francis A. Fahy, 'The Bog Road, Lisdoonvarna' from *The Ould Plaid Shawl and Other Songs* (Dublin, 1949)

THE BIG HOUSE

HE NOT ONLY KNEW every hound in his pack, but he knew their ages, their sires and their dams; and the sires and the dams of most of their sires and dams. He knew the constitution of each, and to what extent their noses were to be trusted. 'It's a very heavy scent to-day,' he would say, 'because Gaylap carries it over the plough. It's only a catching scent because the drops don't hang on the bushes.' His lore on all such matters was incredible, but he would never listen to any argument. A man had a right to his own opinion; but then the man who differed from him knew nothing. He gave out his little laws to favoured individuals; not by way of conversation, for which he cared nothing, but because it might be well that the favoured individual should know the truth on that occasion.

As a man to ride he was a complete master of his art. There was nothing which a horse could do with a man on his back, which Daly could not make him do; and when he had ridden a horse he would know exactly what was within his power. But there was no desire with him for the showing off of a horse. He often rode to sell a horse, but he never seemed to do so. He never rode at difficult places unless driven to do so by the exigencies of the moment. He was always quiet in the field, unless when driven to express himself as to the faults of some young man. Then he could blaze forth in his anger with great power. He was constantly to be seen trotting along a road when hounds were running, because he had no desire to achieve for himself a character for hard riding. But he was always with his hounds when he was wanted, and it was boasted of him that he had ridden four days a week through the season on three horses, and had never lamed one of them. He was rarely known to have a second horse out, and when he did so, it was for some purpose peculiar to the day's work. On such days he had generally a horse to sell.

It is hardly necessary to say that Black Daly was an unmarried man. No one who knew him could conceive that he should have had a wife. His hounds were his children, and he could have taught no wife to assist him in looking after them, with the constant attention and tender care which was given to them by Barney Smith, his hunstman. A wife, had she seen to the feeding of the numerous babies, would have given them too much to eat, and had she not undertaken this care, she would have been useless at Daly's Bridge. But Barney Smith was invaluable; double the amount of work got usually from a huntsman was done by him.There was no kennel man, no second horseman, no stud-groom at the Ahaseragh kennels. It may be said that Black Daly filled all these positions himself, and that in each Barney Smith was his first lieutenant. Circumstances had given him the use of the Ahaseragh kennels, which had been the property of his cousin, and circumstances had not enabled him to build others at Daly's Bridge. Gradually he had found it easier to move himself than the hounds. And so it had come to pass that two rooms had been prepared for him close to the kennels,

and that Mr. Barney Smith gave him such attendance as was necessary. Of strictly personal attendance Black Daly wanted very little; but the discomforts of that home, while one pair of breeches were supposed to be at Daly's Bridge, and the others at Ahaseragh, were presumed by the world at large to be very grievous.

But the personal appearance of Mr. Daly on hunting mornings, was not a matter of indifference. It was not that he wore beautiful pink tops, or came out guarded from the dust by little aprons, or had his cravat just out of the bandbox, or his scarlet coat always new, and in the latest fashion, nor had his hat just come from the shop in Piccadilly with the newest twist to its rim. But there was something manly, and even powerful about his whole apparel. He was always the same, so that by men even in his own county, he would hardly have been known in other garments. The strong, broad-brimmed high hat, with the cord passing down his back beneath his coat, that had known the weather of various winters; the dark, red coat, with long swallow tails, which had grown nearly black under many storms; the dark, buff striped waistcoat, with the stripes running downwards, long, so as to come well down over his breeches; the breeches themselves, which were always of leather, but which had become nearly brown under the hands of Barney Smith or his wife, and the mahogany top-boots, of which the tops seemed to be a foot in length, could none of them have been worn by any but Black Daly. His very spurs must have surely been made for him, they were in length and weight, and general strength of leather, so peculiarly his own. He was unlike other masters of hounds in this, that he never carried a horn; but he spoke to his hounds in a chirruping voice, which all County Galway believed to be understood by every hound in the pack.

Anthony Trollope, *The Land-leaguers*, (London, 1883)

Previous page: *Capt. Blake, Tower Hill, Co Mayo* [*Wynne Collection, Castlebar*]

The Meet, Co Mayo [*Wynne Collection, Castlebar*]

ANTHONY TROLLOPE (1815-1882) Trollope's first writing was done in Ireland when as postal surveyor he was responsible for the provision of Ireland's first pillar-boxes. *The Landleaguers*, published postumously in 1883 is set in Galway.

The Anglo-Irish tradition of hunting packs was established in the mid-eighteenth-century. It was particularly popular in East Galway where the loose stone walls provided good sport. The most famous hunt was The Galway Blazers (the County Galway Hunt) who may have got their name from the time they set fire to Dooly's Hotel in Birr, when they were the guests of the Ormond Hunt.

THE May fire once on every dreaming hill
All the fair land with burning bloom would fill:
All the fair land, at visionary night,
Gave loving glory to the Lord of Light.
Have we no leaping flames of Beltaine praise
To kindle in the joyous ancient ways;
No fire of song, of vision, of white dream,
Fit for the Master of the Heavenly Gleam;
For him who first made Ireland move in chime,
Musical from the misty dawn of time?

Ah, yes: for sacrifice this night we bring
The passion of a lost soul's triumphing:
All rich with faery airs that, wandering long
Uncaught, here gather into Irish song;
Sweet as the old remembering winds that wail
From hill to hill of gracious Inisfail;
Sad as the unforgetting winds that pass
Over her children in her holy grass
At home, and sleeping well upon her breast,
Where snowy Déidre and her sorrows rest.

Another tale we tell you: how a man,
Filled with high dreams, his race of longing ran,
Haunted by fair and infinite desire;
Whose life was music, yet a wounding fire.
Stern is the story: welcome it no less,
Aching and lofty in its loveliness.
Come, then, and keep with us an Irish feast,
Wherein the Lord of Light and Song is priest;
Now, at this opening of the gentle May,
Watch warring passions at their storm and play;
Wrought with the flaming ecstasy of art,
Sprung from the dreaming of an Irish heart.

Lionel Johnson

The stables, Rockingham [Lawrence Collection, National Library of Ireland]

Prologue to *The Countess Cathleen* and *The Heather Field, in Beltaine*: The organ of the Irish Literary Theatre
(Dublin 1899) p.5.

Moore Hall, Co. Mayo [Lawrence Collection, National Library of Ireland]

LIONEL JOHNSON was born in Broadstairs, Kent in 1867. A friend of Yeats from Rhymers' Club days, he lived up to the fin-de-siécle reputation of dying young, a catholic, and of drink (1902). Influenced by Yeats and West of Ireland atmosphere, he was the appropriate man to write the verse prologue to the first programme of the Irish Literary Theatre which presented on May 8, 1899, *The Countess Cathleen* by Mr Yeats and on May 9 *The Heather Field* by Mr Martyn.

Moore Hall, burned down in the Civil War was the home of George Henry Moore, the father of the famous George Augustus, part of whose contribution to the Irish Literary Theatre was the 'doctoring' of Edward Martyn's rather ungainly plays for the stage. The father was that rather anomalous creature a catholic landlord who was able to nurse his tenants through the famine years when they could pay not rents because of his winning £10,000 on his horse Coranna in the Chester Cup in 1846. HIs mercurial son was a very special kind of absentee landlord, refusing to forsake the artists colony in Paris for his paternal acres in Mayo.

The light of evening, Lissadell,
Great windows, open to the south,
Two girls in silk kimonos, both
Beautiful, one a gazelle.
But a raving autumn shears
Blossom from the summer's wreath;
The older is condemned to death,
Pardoned, drags out lonely years
Conspiring among the ignorant.
I know not what the younger dreams —
Some vague Utopia — and she seems,
When withered old and skeleton-gaunt,
An image of such politics.
Many a time I think to seek
One or the other out and speak
Of that old Georgian mansion, mix
Pictures of the mind, recall
That table and the talk of youth,
Two girls in silk kimonos, both
Beautiful, one a gazelle.

Dear shadows, now you know it all,
All the folly of a fight
With a common wrong or right.
The innocent and the beautiful
Have no enemy but time;
Arise and bid me strike a match
And strike another till time catch;
Should the conflagration climb,
Run till all the sages know.
We the great gazebo built,
They convicted us of guilt;
Bid me strike a match and blow.

October 1927

W. B. Yeats, In memory of Eva Gore-Booth and Con Markiewicz, from *The Winding Stair and Other Poems* (London 1933)

  THE POLLEXFENS were at best small gentry so the young Yeats would not have visited Lissadell House as part of his social round, but he had always admired the house which he could see from Rosses Point. When in 1894 he was invited to lecture at the school house on the estate, he met Eva Gore-Booth and her even more beautiful sister Con, whom he fancied looked like Maud Gonne. The pleasure of those days when he had his first taste of the 'accustomed, ceremonious' life remained with him always so that thirty years afterwards he could still remember these 'comets'.

54 Certainly they influenced his life and work and led him to take the first steps on the road to Coole.

Eva and Constance Gore-Booth Co-operating. (Kilgannon Collection, Sligo Museum) **55**

ONE REMEMBERS EVERYTHING better than the moment of ecstasy - the colour of the rooms, their shapes, the furniture, all is seen by me to-day as truly as if the reality were before me; the very wood we burned in the great fireplace, the shapes of one log, how it fell into ashes at one end leaving a great knotted stump at the other, the moving of the candles into shadowy places so that the light should not fall upon our eyes - all these details are remembered, only the moment of ecstasy is forgotten. It is a pity that this is so. But I remember how I stood at the foot of the bed bidding her good-night, for the moment comes when all lovers must part, unless indeed they are married folk 'who occupy the same room.' The occupation of the same room, one of the most important questions in love's economy, was being treated when the pink waiter brought in our dinner; and the reader will remember that I was telling Doris how those learned in love had told me that he who has not waked up in the morning with his beloved seeing the sunlight in the window, hearing the birds in the branches, does not know the rapture of love, the enchantment of its intimacy. The sympathetic reader will not have forgotten this avowal, and his instinct leaping forward he will have seen me standing triumphant on the summit of all earthly love; therefore the admission that, feeling myself falling asleep, I bade Doris good-night at the foot of the bed will have cast him into the slough of despond from which my narrative, however lively it may prove, may fail to lift him. But though I did not realise the sacred moment at Orelay, and consequently will never realise it, in this world at least, that moment which, with the music of harps, Wagner depicts so completely, when Siegfried's kiss awakes Brunnhilde and she opens her eyes to the beauty of the world, I learned nevertheless at Orelay that my friend who said I was but a novice, a mere acolyte in Love's service, was not wholly wrong in his criticism of my life, for waking suddenly after sleeping for some hours, I heard Doris trying the handle of my door, and I called to ask her if she were seeking anything. She said she wished to know the time; there was no clock in her room, but there was one on my chimney-piece. It seemed so kind of her to come to my room that I could not refrain from taking her in my arms, and I told her that I had never seen a woman so early in the morning before. This pleased her, for she did not wish our love to be sullied with memories of other women. She shed such a delight about me that morning that I sought her the following morning in her room, and that visit, too, is remembered, though it is less distinct in my mind than her visit to my room. When I left her to dress myself she came running in to tell me something she had forgotten to tell me, and she sat watching me while I shaved, laughing at the absurdity, for it was absurd that she should always have something to say to me. No sooner had she gone than something awoke in my mind too, something I had unfortunately forgotten to say, and I had to rush back and to beg of her to let me open the door, though she was in her bath.

56

Right: *The Library, Renvyle Hotel, Co. Galway*

GEORGE AUGUSTUS MOORE was born at his father's house Moore Hall, Lough Carra, Co. Mayo in 1852. *Enfant terrible* of the Irish Renaissance, gadfly of 'dear Edward' Martyn, his account of his Irish adventure in *Hail and Farewell* (1914) makes very entertaining if scandalously inaccurate reading. His most significant Irish works are *The Untilled Field* (1902) — a seminal collection of short-stories, deliberate models for the new Irish writers, and *The Lake* (1905).

In his preface to the 1914 edition of *The Untilled Field* he writes, 'It must have been somewhere at the end of the nineties, not unlikely in ninety-nine, that dear Edward said to me in the Temple: 'I should like to write my plays in Irish.' And it was not long afterwards, in the beginning of 1900, that Yeats persuaded him to come to Ireland to found a literary theatre. In search of a third person, they called on me in

I know a statue of a woman leaning forward wiping her thighs, and that was the movement I discovered Doris in. The statue is a stupid thing, lacking in personal observation; all that the sculptor had omitted I perceived in Doris, but the comparison only floated across my mind; the delight of seeing her naked absorbed me, and I thought of other things, of Fragonard, for Fragonard realised what a little thing a woman is compared with a man, and this was just the idea that Doris conveyed; her great mass of hair made her look smaller than she really was, her head seemed too large for her body, yet this seeming, for it was no more than a seeming, did not detract from her beauty; she was as charming as if she had looked the regulation seven-and-a-half heads, for she was a Fragonard - an eighteenth century bedfellow, that is what she was . . . She bid me away. No one had ever seen her in her bath before; she did not like it; no, she did not! And thinking how charming these subterfuges were, how little love would be without them, I heard her calling, saying that she would be with me in ten minutes, that I was to ring and tell the waiter to bring up our first breakfast.

George Moore, *Memoirs of my Dead Life*, (London, 1906), pp 207-8

Victoria Street, and it is related in *Ave** how we packed our bags and went away to do something. We all did something, but none did what he set out to do. Yeats founded a realistic theatre, Edward emptied two churches — he and Palestrina between them — and I wrote *The Untilled Field*, a book written in the beginning out of no desire of self-expression, but in the hope of furnishing the young Irish of the future with models.'

The Lake is less naturalistic and much more consciously symbolic. When the priest-hero dives in the lake to come out on the other bank lay and free, it is obviously Ireland he is washing off him as much as his celibacy. Even here Moore's sense of mischief did not desert him; he called his hero Oliver Gogarty, another oblique claim to literary fame for the Buck Mulligan of *Ulysses*. He died on January 21, 1933 in his famous Ebury Street house in Victoria.

*The first of the three volume, Ave, Salve, Vale of *Hail and Farewell*

LORD SHRULE, *an elderly benevolent-looking man dressed in a somewhat old-fashioned riding costume*, MILES TYRRELL, *and* CARDEN TYRRELL *enter by the door at right.*

LORD SHRULE: Now that the inspector has gone out again to his work, I must say, my dear Carden, I am astounded at hearing of this new expenditure you contemplate. I did not like to speak before him — Ah, Ussher, how do you do? (*To* KIT.) And how is my little man?

KIT: (*Holding out his hand.*): Very well, thanks —

LORD SHRULE: That's right, that's right. I was saying, my dear Carden, your fresh project of expenditure fills me with amazement. Have you heard about it, Ussher?

USSHER: I have indeed.

LORD SHRULE: Well, does it not seem to you extremely imprudent — nay, reckless?

USSHER: Oh, you must not ask me, Lord Shrule. Carden seems determined. And, after all, he is the best judge of his own affairs.

TYRRELL: Yes, Barry, that is just it.

LORD SHRULE: Come, come, Carden, you will not mind the advice of an old man who has a long experience in the management of land. Your father and I were always fast friends, and I naturally take a great interest in you and your family.

TYRRELL: I know you have always been very kind, Lord Shrule. Forgive me if I have spoken hastily. I did not mean —

LORD SHRULE: Of course not, my dear Carden — I quite understand you. I fear indeed you must think it rather impertinent of your friends to interfere in your business. But then, as I have said, I consider myself privileged.

TYRRELL: You may be quite sure, Lord Shrule, I could not take anything from you except in good part.

LORD SHRULE: I thought so. Well, let me implore of you, if only for the sake of your family, to desist. This is certainly the wildest scheme I ever heard of, and couldn't pay, even if the drainage were to turn out a success.

TYRRELL: But you forget it is necessary now that the drainage of the heather field falls into this land. There is the cutting through it for the water to get to the sea. Now, what is easier than to reclaim the land through which this cutting goes?

LORD SHRULE: My dear Carden, don't mind the cutting — don't mind the heather field. What you have only got to think of is to cease altogether from loading your estate with an ever-growing burden of debt. For goodness' sake leave these works alone. If you continue them you will simply beggar yourself.

TYRRELL: (*Uneasily.*): I do not see that at all. The work will be very remunerative. It will double the value of the estate.

LORD SHRULE: Oh, Carden listen to me. I know well the nature of such works as you are carrying on. I have tried them myself — on a far smaller scale, of course. They never repay their expenditure.

TYRRELL: That is a mere assertion unsupported by argument. On the other hand, I have excellent reasons why I should believe that what I am about to undertake must have the best results. Look at the rich pasture now in the heather field. And am I to suppose that I shall not have the same in the valley when it is reclaimed? Until you can prove logically that I am mistaken, I must continue those works, which I clearly see are so profitable. Am I not right, Barry?

USSHER: I have said I shall never again discourage you, Carden.

LORD SHRULE: Ussher, upon my word I thought you knew better. But I suppose it is useless remonstrating with our friend about his experiments, which amount to seeming mania.

Edward Martyn, *The Heather Field* (produced Dublin, 1899)

EDWARD MARTYN was born at Masonbrook, Loughrea in 1859. He became co-founder and namer of the Irish Literary Theatre. Certainly the most generous and cultured of the group, his knowledge of European art and theatre was put at the disposal of his wilder colleagues, Moore and Yeats. Like Moore he was a catholic landlord with a house Tulira Castle in south Galway (an ancestor had been exempted from the Penal Laws) and he bore the expenses of launching the venture that was to become the Abbey Theatre. He was much more at the mercy of his conscience and consequently much more susceptible to attacks upon the 'immortality' of such plays as *The Countess Cathleen*. His own play (after Ibsen) *The Heather Field* followed *The Countess Cathleen* on the second night (May 9, 1899) as the first presentations of The Irish Literary Theatre at the Antient Concert Rooms in Brunswick (now Pearse) Street Dublin. When the Abbey went popular and realistic he founded his own amateur company, The Hardwicke Street Theatre where he staged the first Dublin productions of Chekov, Strindberg and Ibsen. His other great contribution to Irish cultural life was the advocacy of church music, especially that of Palestrina, and the establishment of the annual Féis Ceóil in 1897. He died in 1923 after willing his body for research.

The Earl of Lucan at Castlebar 1895 (Wynne Collection)

The Bingham family became Earls of Lucan in 1795 and took as their motto, 'Spes Mea Christus.' The subject of the photograph is the Third Earl who owned in all 60,000 acres in Mayo. A visiting journalist remarked in 1881 that he was absent too often, that his home farm was not well-managed and that his town of Castlebar was badly developed.

Hooker (centre picture) owned by the Healy brothers, Galway Harbour, 1894

TOWNS

"IF THESE are your views your mother will have to think of something else for you, Martha."

"I was up in Conarchy's shop yesterday," Martha Lee went on, "taking it all in. There were people there having themselves fitted out. Some of them were emigrants. I waited, observing the milliner attending them, imagining myself in her place. One party in a shawl, stout and with a little wobble in the walk - she came in like this" — Martha took a little comical trot down the room — "leaned across the counter and whispered to the milliner, and the milliner whispered back. They began to nod and smile and agree with each other, and I thought in the end they would fall into each other's arms and kiss. 'But the shape - what kind of a shape would we be saying?' the milliner asked sweetly at last. The stout party gave her a thump in the neck. 'You're a devil, I hear, for the Paris fashions,' says she, 'but you'll not make a show of me, for when I do wear a headpiece I do like to feel that it has a good hoult of me. Now give me out a nice bonnet with good jawstrings to it.''

Ellen Noonan could not keep serious any longer. Martha Lee's mimicries were too good.

"When the stout party had gone with her handbox," Martha Lee went on, 'a couple of young chits from the town came fluttering in. They wore their hats on the last angle of their polls - airy pieces got up to look as if the next chance breeze that blew would waft them all up to the heavens. They were giggling, or trying to suppress giggling, as they stood at the counter. One of the party addressed the milliner in an accent that sounded as if the Reverend Mother had just handed it out over the wall of the most select boarding school in the land for young ladies of high breeding. They had to pull down all the boxes in the place for the inspection of the young ladies. The whole stock-in-trade of the shop was reviewed, and then they bought a pennyworth of elastic, and went giggling out of the shop. They were followed by a family which was sending one of its daughters to Philadelphia from her mountain home. Her face was as hard as a board, her light brown hair lay in little lumps about her head, wisps of it streeling down her face. She looked exactly as if her clothes were bundled about her and tied in the middle with a rope - a sack of a slovenly, pugnacious-looking agricultural apparition. It was the very devil to please her. She stood viewing herself in the mirror, a hat with a blaze of colours lying lop-sided on her head. 'Do you like it?' asked one of her friends. 'I do and I don't,' she said. 'I think I'd like something livelier.' Then her mother said: 'Julia, it's crooked. Give it a twisht more to the wesht.'''

Ellen Noonan laughed until the bed shook under her at the scathing tongue, the splendid acting of the other. Then she shook her head.

"You won't do as a milliner, Martha," she said.

Martha Lee paced up and down the room, her hands behind her back, a magnificent-looking, angry pantheress.

Seamus O'Kelly, *Wet Clay*, (Dublin, 1919) pp 118-19

Right.*Wynne's Photography Shop, Loughrea* Left: *House next door* (*Wynne Collection, Castlebar*)

(*A man carrying an antique camera with its trivet and black cloth enters through the gate. He has a beard and sharp eyes behind spectacles.*)

PHOTOGRAPHER (*to* CRILLY): I'm not mistaken, am I, in figuring that an important event is taking place here to-day? (*Leaving down the apparatus he takes a professional look at the yard and the persons.*) Confirmations, Confraternity Meetings, Ordinations, Weddings — I record them in my own special manner. Single photograph one shilling and sixpence, group two shillings and sixpence. I am Bartholomew Vincent Murann, Photographer to the Maharajah of Judpur.

CRILLY: That's a long way off.

MURANN: I travel. Recently I was where His Highness and suite were on a liner bound for the United States. They stepped on Irish ground. He gave me his patronage then. (*Turning to* CRILLY *with an album.*) You'll find the photographs there, sir. (CRILLY *takes album.*) I thought I might take the photograph here before the assembling of the First Communion class.

CRILLY: What photograph?

MURANN: The new Master of the Workhouse.

CRILLY: 'Pon my word, you fellows are ready for the drop kick! He has only been appointed.

MURANN: First day in office! Something to show in the parlour in after years! Ah, what a wonderful thing is the camera! What it can hand down to posterity! — And so reasonable in price!

TOURNOUR: I'll get my own likeness taken at the reasonable price of one and sixpence.

CRILLY: A picture of Tournour, no less!

TOURNOUR: To put in the Ward Master's office.

CRILLY: Office?

TOURNOUR: If there isn't an office, I'll get one.

CRILLY (*in disgust*): Give him the Workhouse!

MURANN: What a picturesque nook this is! A setting indeed! The grey old walls! The massive doorway! Something that's like . . . Well, well, who knows what it's like? If there was some figure there!

(THOMAS MUSKERRY *comes on the steps.*) By Jove, that's it! That's it! The Master!

CRILLY: Not the Master you want.

MURANN (*to* MUSKERRY): Stay, sir! Don't move!
(MUSKERRY *in astonishment keeps his position.*)

CRILLY: HE's retired — he's not Master any more.

MURANN: He's the proper figure for the Master, standing there! Oh, sir, would you keep your stand just for a minute. A photograph of you is required!
(*He sets up his apparatus.*)

MUSKERRY: May I ask who you are, sir?

MURANN: Bartholomew Vincent Murann, photographer at large.

MUSKERRY: Has this been ordered?
(*The photographer is now busy getting black cloth over his head and the camera.*)

MUSKERRY: The Guardians aren't as neglectful as I thought.

TOURNOUR: At one-and-sixpence to you, Mister Muskerry.
(MUSKERRY *notices him but says nothng.* CRILLY *opens the album that had been given him.*)

MURANN: The Maharajah and his suite. And passengers from our port on the gangway.

CRILLY: Passengers! I'd like to see myself amongst them!

MURANN: Splendid position! Just a little to the right. I'll have you dominate the prospect.
(*Under the black cloth there are hurried movements.* CHRISTY CLARKE *enters wheeling a barrow.* CRILLY *finds something in the album that startles him.*)

CRILLY: God in heaven! What am I looking at? It isn't Covey! On the gangway of a liner for America! If that's him, it will be the end of me!
(*The photographer comes from under the black cloth.*)

MURANN: I'm proud, sir, proud of having the opportunity of obtaining such a striking photograph. It will be looked on as a work of art. There you are, a majestic figure, if I may say so, with the wall of the establishment you officiated in at your back. A worthy memento this will be!

MUSKERRY: The Board of Guardians can put under it what was publically stated — "The pattern of officials of Ireland."
TOURNOUR: Maybe they will and maybe they won't.
MUSKERRY (*coming to him*): Tournour!
TOURNOUR: Humbly asking the pardon of the retired Master of Garrisowen Workhouse!!

Padraic Colum, 'Thomas Muskerry' in *Plays* (Dublin 1966)

PADRAIC COLUM was born in Longford in 1881 and was son of the workhouse master of that town. Now known, perhaps unfortunately, as the author of such heavily-anthologised pieces as *The Old Woman of the Roads*, *A Drover*, and *Cradle Song*, since they have obscured his fame as dramatist and folklorist. He was one of the earliest of the Abbey playwrights and his play *Thomas Muskerry* (1909) was one of those which determined the theatre's future as a home of naturalistic drama. Most of his later life was spent in America. He died in 1972.

Castlebar Asylum Attendants, 1898 (Wynne Collection)

65

HE REACHED THE MARKET town while it was yet morning. He led the creel of turf through the straggling streets, where some people with the sleep in their eyes were moving about. The only sound he made was a low word of encouragement to the donkey.

"How much for the creel?" a man asked, standing at his shop door.

"Six shilling," Denis Donohoe replied, and waited, for it was above the business of a decent turf-seller to praise his wares or press for a sale.

"Good luck to you, son," said the merchant, "I hope you'll get it." He smiled, folded his hands one over the other, and retired to his shop.

Denis Donohoe moved on, saying in an undertone to the donkey, "Gee-up, Patsy. That old fellow is no good."

There were other inquiries, but nobody purchased. They said that money was very scarce. Denis Donohoe said nothing; money was too remote a thing for him to imagine how it could be ever anything else except scarce. He grew tired of going up and down past shops where there was no sign of business, so he drew the side streets and laneways, places where children screamed about the road, where there was a scent of soapy water, where women came to their doors and looked at him with eyes that expressed a slow resentment, their arms bare above the elbows, their hair hanging dankly about their ears, their voices, when they spoke, monotonous, and always sounding a note of tired complaint.

On the rise of a little bridge Denis Donohoe met a red-haired woman, a family of children skirmishing about her; there was a battle light in her wolfish eyes, her idle hands were folded over her stomach.

"How much, gossoon?" she asked.

"Six shilling."

"Six devils!" She walked over to the creel, handling some of the sods of turf. Denis Donohoe knew she was searching a constitutionally abusive mind for some word contemptuous of his wares. She found it at last, for she smacked her lips. It was in the Gaelic.

"*Spairteach*!" she cried - a word that was eloquent of bad turf, stuff dug from the first layer of the bog, a mere covering for the correct vein beneath it.

"It's good stone turf," Denis Donohoe protested, a little nettled.

The woman was joined by some people who were hanging about, anxious to take part in bargaining which involved no personal liability. They argued, made jokes, shouted, and finally began to bully Denis Donohoe, the woman leading, her voice half a scream, her stomach heaving, her eyes dancing with excitement, a yellow froth gathering at the corners of her angry mouth, her hand gripping a sod of the turf, for the only dissipation life now offered her was this haggling with and shouting down of turf sellers. Denis Donohoe stood immovable beside his cart, patient as his donkey, his swarthy face stolid under the shadow of his broad-brimmed black hat, his intelligent eyes quietly measuring his noisy antagonists. When the woman's anger had quite spent itself the turf was purchased for five shillings.

Séumas O'Kelly, *Waysiders* (Dublin, 1917) pp 42-45

SÉUMAS O'KELLY born in Loughrea Co. Galway in 1881, is chiefly remembered nowadays as the author of the story *The Weaver' Grave* which as a radio play by Micheal O hAodha won the Italia Prize in 1961, but in his time was an active Nationalist journalist, friend of Arthur Griffith, pre-Abbey realistic dramatist, short-story writer and novelist. His best play, The *Shuiler's Child* anticipates such melodramas as *The Year of the Hiker*. His death in November 1918, after harrassment by British soldiers, has caused him to be regarded as a martyr for the cause and he was honoured by a national funeral. *Wet Clay*, his best novel, was published posthumously in 1919.

Waysiders, subtitled 'Stories of Connacht', contains some of O'Kelly's best stories. Though a Nationalist in politics he had no illusions about the realities of Irish life and his clear view of the drudgery of farm life anticipates Brinsley MacNamara and Paddy Kavanagh.

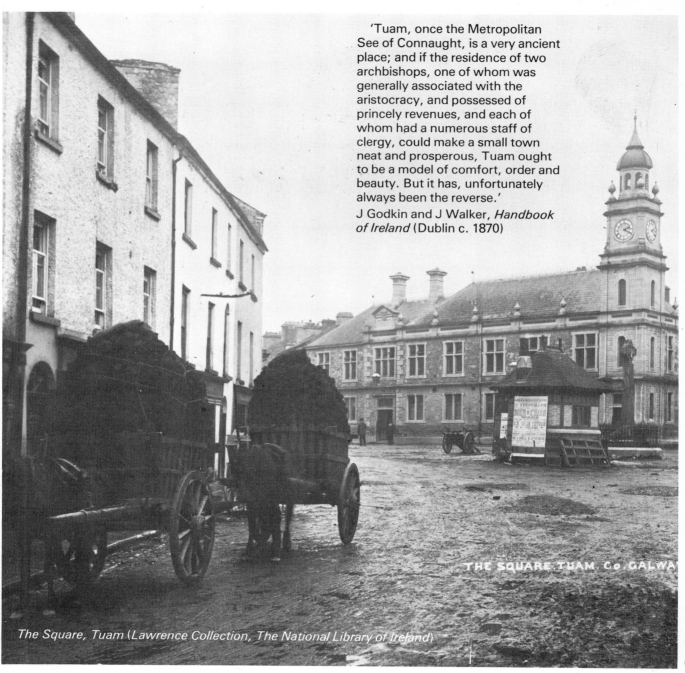

'Tuam, once the Metropolitan
See of Connaught, is a very ancient
place; and if the residence of two
archbishops, one of whom was
generally associated with the
aristocracy, and possessed of
princely revenues, and each of
whom had a numerous staff of
clergy, could make a small town
neat and prosperous, Tuam ought
to be a model of comfort, order and
beauty. But it has, unfortunately
always been the reverse.'

J Godkin and J Walker, *Handbook
of Ireland* (Dublin c. 1870)

THE SQUARE, TUAM, Co GALWAY

The Square, Tuam (Lawrence Collection, The National Library of Ireland)

67

Castle Street, Sligo (Lawrence Collection, National Library of Ireland)

Mary Davenport O'Neill was the wife of Joseph O'Neill the novelist. Born in Galway in 1893 she has written verse plays as well as poetry. The poem 'Galway' is strictly speaking outside our period, but that part of the city is so timeless, and the poem so evocative, that we could not exclude it.

SWIFTLY WE GLIDE over the salt water estuary of Lough Athalia, into the great terminus of Galway, at 1.45 o'clock, and out through it into the enormous limestone hotel, built, 'regardless of expense' by the original directors of the railway; and from whence, 'after a bit and a sup', we emerge among the beggars into Eyre Square, surrounded by hotels, club-houses, banks, private residences and coach offices, where the great 'Bian' can forward us 'anywhere', and in which we can choose our newspaper according to our politics or polemics.''

Sir William Wilde: *Lough Corrib* (Dublin 1967)

Right: *Eyre Square, Galway (Lawrence Collection, National Library of Ireland)*

The monument is to Lord Dunkellin and was erected in 1873 and removed in 1922. As often, in 'spontaneous demonstration of affection', the tenants were forced by levy to contribute.

EDITH SOMERVILLE was born in Corfu in 1858 but apart from deliberately undertaken tours for the purposes of collecting copy spent most of her life in Munster and Connacht. She was the quintessential Anglo-Irish centaur and was the extravert partner of the two. *Violet Martin* was born at Ross, Co. Galway in 1862. More aware of John Bull's Other Ireland than Edith who lived in quasi-English close quarters in Castletownshend, Co. Cork, she supplied the depth, the gothic element and the self-critical humour. Their most famous books, *The Irish RM Stories* began simply as hunting sketches but developed into pieces of social history. Their finest novel, *The Real Charlotte* was published in three volumes in 1894. Edith continued to write after Violet's death of cancer in 1915 and still used the imprint Somerville and Ross, claiming that Violet's spirit was constantly with her. Attempts to form the same kind of non-physical passionate friendship with Dame Ethel Smyth did not succeed. She died at Castletownshend in 1949.

Market Day, Clifden, Lawrence Collection (*National Library of Ireland*)

"WHOEVER SAYS thim throuts isn't leppin' fresh out o' the lake he's a dom liar, and it's little I think of tellin' it t'ye up to yer nose! There's not one in the counthry but knows yer thricks and yer chat, and ye may go home out o' that, with yer bag sthrapped round ye, and ye can take the tay-leaves and the dhrippin' from the servants, and huxther thim to feed yer cats, but thanks be to God ye'll take nothing out o' my basket this day!"

There was a titter of horrified delight from the crowd.

"Ye never spoke a truer word than that, Mary Norris," replied a voice that sent a chill down Christopher's back; "When I come into Lismoyle, it's not to buy rotten fish from a drunken fish-fag, that'll be begging for crusts at my halldoor to-morrow. If I hear another word out of yer mouth I'll give you and your fish to the police, and the streets'll be rid of you and yer infernal tongue for a week, at all events, and the prison'll have a treat that it's pretty well used to!"

Another titter rewarded this sally, and Charlotte, well pleased, turned to walk away. As she did so, she caught sight of Christopher, looking at her with an expression from which he had not time to remove his emotions, and for a moment she wished that the earth would open and swallow her up. She reddened visibly, but recovered herself, and at once made her way out into the street towards him.

"How are you again, Mr. Dysart? You just came in time to get a specimen of the *res angusta domi*," she said, in a voice that contrasted almost ludicrously with her last utterances. "People like David, who talk about the advantages of poverty, have probably never tried buying fish in Lismoyle. It's always the way with these drunken old hags. They repay your charity by impudence and bad language, and one has to speak pretty strongly to them to make one's meaning penetrate to their minds."

Her eyes were still red and swollen from her violent crying at the funeral. But for them, Christopher could hardly have believed that this was the same being whom he had last seen on the sofa at Tally Ho, with the black gloves and the sal volatile.

"Oh yes, of course," he said vaguely; "everyone has to undergo Mary Norris some time or other. If you are going back to Tally Ho now, I can drive you there."

"No thank you, Mr Dysart. I'm not done my marketing yet, but Francie's at home and she'll give you tea. Don't wait for me. I've no appetite for anything to-day. I only came out to get a mouthful of fresh air, in hopes it might give me a better night, though, indeed, I've small chance of it after what I've gone through."

Christopher drove on, and tried not to think of Miss Mullen or of his mother or Pamela, while his too palpably discreet hostess elbowed her way through the crowd in the opposite direction.

Somerville and Ross *The Real Charlotte* (London 1894)

The Fish Market, Galway, seen from the west with the Spanish Arch in the background and the old Claddagh Footbridge. (Lawrence Collection, National Library of Ireland)

SUDDENLY A MELODIOUS STRAIN floated out over the sunlit water, and the music of a delicious female voice carolling a Celtic song was borne on the air.

It was a simple, artless song, a quaint old Irish ballad telling of the sorrowful loves of a certain fair MacDermott and a certain dark O'Rourke, and yet the enchantress Lurline, seated on her mossy rock beside the Rhine, could scarce have poured forth a more tender and bewitching melody than this, which seemed like the harmony of silver bells tinkled by music-loving fairies in some bosky dell beside the water.

The melody proceeded from beneath the shade of a magnificent sycamore that grew on the verge of the shore. There, on the trunk of a prostrate tree, were seated an old man and a maiden, and it was from the red lips of the latter that the stream of song was flowing.

The old man, who wore the high conical cap (or *fileadh*) and flowing robes of an Irish bard, was a venerable, white-haired patriarch, with a majesty akin to that of one of the giant trees of the primeval wood that stood at his back, robed with trailing ivy and hoary with moss. Manus O'Cuirnin had long followed the profession of seanachie — a combination of bard, story-teller, and historian — and his was long the place of honour at the feasts of the neighbouring Irish chieftains. But now his palsied fingers refused to touch the harp-strings as they had been wont, his shoulders were bowed with the weight of nigh a century, and he who had seen generation after generation pass away lived in daily and almost hourly expectation of the summons which was to open to him the the the gates of another world. He had had two sons, both of whom were gone before him to the grave: one perishing in the war in Flanders, the other dying at home. The latter had left two children, a son and a daughter, the daughter being the fair young songstress who now sat by her grandsire's side.

Despite the seanachie's great age his sight was almost unimpaired, and he was now poring over an old yellow manuscript. It was only when the maiden's song ceased that he raised his eyes from the black lines of Celtic characters.

"Gillamachree," he said, turning to his young companion, "I feel as if I were thirty years younger when I listen to your sweet voice, and the blood runs right warmly through my old veins. You remind me of the bird whose singing raised St. Fursey to the gate of heaven. What would I do at all without you, avourneen?"

He laid his feeble hand caressingly on her head. A dainty, graceful little head it was — a head crowned

PATRICK G. SMYTH was born in Ballina in 1857 and became a teacher before emigrating to America and a life of journalism. His verse and novels are nineteenth-century romantic and like Lily MacManus and Grace Rhys he turned to earlier happier periods in Irish history for his plots. *King and Viking* (1889) was about the Norse invasions and his best-known novel, wildly popular at the time of publication, *The Wild Rose of Lough Gill* (1904) dealt with the brief bright glory of Owen Roe O'Neill. It is rather romantic and sentimental by modern tastes. Influenced by the newly formed Gaelic League and residual Connacht usage he incorporates many Irish words in his text.

with the natural "glory of woman," a wealth of hair that, bound by the simple ribbon of maidenhood, streamed down the owner's back in a mass of glossy brown tresses. She was barely sixteen, a brunette, and singularly handsome. Her beauty was of that sweet, piquant, peculiarly Celtic type that is so racy of the Irish soil. A perfect embodiment she looked of fresh young health, of gazelle-like grace and vigour — and the spirit of the seanachie's grandchild was pure as the wholesome air that breathed around her.

A shawl of dark woollen stuff was gracefully draped round her shoulders and fastened on one of them by a silver brooch representing a cluster of interwined serpents. Old Manus was dressed in his particoloured costume of Irish bard; and the pair made a quite picturesque little group — a group very suggestive of May and December.

"Now, grandfather mine," she replied, with a light laugh, "I fear you have too high an opinion of me. You praise my singing — you who taught me how to sing, ay, and to play your clairseach, too. You compare me to the bird of St. Fursey. Alas! 'tis not my poor voice can raise your mind to heaven."

"It can, asthore, and so can your face, for your bright eyes make me think of my poor dead Nuala, who is now with the saints — ay, brings her to my memory not as you saw her, ma colleen, a withered old vanithee, but a merry, handsome girl like yourself. Ah, wirrasthrue! wirrasthrue!" continued the old man, mournfully, "that was a long, long time ago. The old people are all gone, acushla, all gone; — but I'll soon follow them, and the gray worn heart shall have rest at last."

Patrick G. Smyth, *The Wild Rose of Lough Gill* (Dublin, 1883) pp2,3.

Killary Harbour Leenane (Lawrence Collection National Library of Ireland)

Going to Hazelwood Races, Sligo [*Kilgannon Collection, Sligo Museum*]

POLITICS

CONSTANCE GORE-BOOTH, later Countess Marciewicz, was the great heroine figure of the 1916 Rising. A very beautiful young woman, she fascinated the young Yeats and sorely disappointed the Anglo-Irish when she espoused the national cause. She was the first woman to be elected to the British House of Commons but did not take her seat. She was Minister for Labour in the Republican Government in 1919.

Constance, Countess Marciewicz, New York 1922 (Sligo Museum)

FLANAGHAN'S FLYING MACHINE

'Twas Flanagan found out the secret of flight,
And made such a perfect affair,
That Farman and Bleriot, Latham and White
Proclaimed him the King o' the air.
And, mind you, I think he deserved his success
For really he worked very hard;
Six days out of seven his private address
Was — the Hospital Accident Ward.
But soon he was safe and serene
And every day could be seen
By admiring crowds,
Leppin' over the clouds
In his marvellous flying machine.

Said the Kaiser — "On Britain I'm going to pounce
Like a terrier dog on a rat".
Said his officers — "Do, and you'll get the grand bounce,
For you're talking too much through your hat."
Said the Kaiser — "There's nothing on earth you'll allow
My army and fleet can defy."
Said his officers — "Nothin' on earth, sire, but how
About something up there in the sky?"
Said the Kaiser — "I know what you mean
Though faith! I'd forgotten it clean,
The war is postponed
While the atmosphere's owned
By Flanaghan's flying machine."

Percy French

One of the characteristic features of Percy French was his total acceptance of modern systems of transport for all their mechanical inefficiency. Such songs as 'Jim Wheelahan's Automobeel' (1903) and 'Maguire's Motor Bike' (1906) were popular with audiences who affected to disregard, envied and in time accepted the new-fangled. 'Flanagan's Flying Machine' written soon after Bleriot's successful English Channel flight, is typical of this happy opportunism.

Royal Flying Corps, Castlebar (*Wynne Collection, Castlebar*)
RFC contingent outside a hangar at Castlebar Aerodrome, late 1917.
Though Baldonnel was the main Irish airfield there were several other bases about the country.

THE VALUE OF PATSY

The old lady had asked to see the recruiting officer, and that functionary was now interviewing her.

"What can I do for you, mother? Want to enlist?" he inquired jocularly.

"Bedad no, sorr," said the visitor. "Oi wants to know whether me bhoy. Patsy has 'listed."

"Patsy Roonan?" asked the officer.

"Yis, sorr."

"Then he joined the Connaught Rangers yesterday."

"Ochone! ochone! Phwat'll Oi do now widout him!" howled Mrs. Roonan.

"Buy him out, mother," suggested the officer.

"Bedad, Oi nivir thought av that!" cried the old lady, producing a purse.

"How much, now, Captain, will yez take for Patsy?"

"Ten pounds is the price," smiled the officer.

"Tin pounds?" shrieked Patsy's mother. "Tin pounds for Patsy! Sure Oi thought a matter av half-a-crown would square it. But tin pounds! Ye've made a bad bargain, Captain, if ye think Patsy's worth that, an' ye can kape him."

THE SOLDIER WHO TURNED

Some time ago I enlisted in a Cavalry Regiment, in which I remained twelve months, recounts a soldier.

Things not being to my liking, however, I managed to secure a suit of "civvies" from a recruit who was sleeping his first night in barracks, and deserted.

I got to Dublin by degrees, and having spent all my money, was on my beam ends. Work and food were not to be had, so for a second time I made my way to the recruiting depot. A sergeant spotted me, and this time I chose The Connaught Rangers.

I had passed the doctor, when I was sent before the Sergeant-Major. The latter asked me the usual questions, which I answered in a straightforward fashion. Then he said, "Turn round, young man," and, not thinking, I "about turned" in soldier fashion, and put both feet into it with regulation click.

After that I put both feet into the guard room.

THE RANGER The journal of the Connaught Rangers (July 1914, Vol.2 No.3) p12.

Renmore Barracks, Galway [Lawrence Collection, National Library of Ireland]

The Military Barracks, Castlebar (Wynne Collection)

County of _Galway ER_   District of _Loughrea_

NAME, *P. J. Kelly*

OCCUPATION. *Farmer*

RESIDENCE, *Grangepark. Killenadeema. Loughrea*

Regᵈ Nᵒ *221*

PHOTOGRAPH

The above is a good likeness

DATE OF DESCRIPTION,	*12 Nov 94*
HEIGHT,	*5* Ft. *7 ¾* In.
AGE,	*45* Years.
Make,	*Medium*
Hair,	*Very dark turning grey*
Eyes,	*Dark grey*
Eyebrows,	*Dark*
Nose,	*Thick. Cocked*
Mouth,	*Broad, thick lips*
Complexion,	*Dark*
Visage,	*Round. high cheek bones*
Whiskers,	*Small side*
Moustache,	*None*
Beard,	*None*
Native Place,	*Killenadeema. Galway*

REMARKS—(*Here insert particulars of eccentric habits. peculiarities of gait, manner, &c., and marks on person*).

Round shoulders & stoops forward when Walking

No. of File.   OBSERVATIONS.

History has been submitted

84

islanders are not portrayed as they might well have been as uncouth, uncivilised people. Her novel *Hurrish* (1886) treats the Land War from the landlord's point of view and her rendering of dialogue is of the Samuel Lover, export-only kind. She is most acceptable to modern taste in her books of quasi-mystical poems. Best of these is *With the Wild Geese* (1902) which includes the sequence 'In the Aran Isles'. She died in 1913.

done for! That was the long and short of it. Everything was at an end. His career wrecked, finished before it had fairly begun. Not in Clare alone, but from one end of Ireland to the other, his name was the signal, he knew, for contempt and execration. Never would any Irish constituency open its doors to receive him; never would his voice be heard in the halls of Westminster, or anywhere nearer home; never would a single one of those visions of success and triumph, upon which he had floated so securely, now come true!

Emily Lawless, *Hurrish* (London, 1886) pp242-244

Dr. Tully's House after eviction, Woodford (Lawrence Collection, National Library of Ireland)

A MONSTER DEMONSTRATION in favour of the Land League movement, which sought to reform the Irish land laws, was held at Straide, County Mayo, on the 1st February, 1880. Mr. Michael Davitt was amongst the speakers, and a peculiar interest was attached to the meeting from the fact that the platform from which he spoke was erected over the very ruins of the old homestead from which he, with his father and mother, had been evicted many years before. On that occasion Mr. Davitt delivered the following speech:-

While every nerve must be strained to stave off, if possible, the horrible fate which befell our famine-slaughtered kindred in 1847 and 1848, the attention of our people must not for a moment be withdrawn from the primary cause of these periodical calamities nor their exertions be relaxed in this great social struggle for the overthrow of the odious system responsible for them. Portions of the English press had recently declared that the charity of Englishmen would be more spontaneous and generous if this agitation did not stand in the way. Well, Ireland's answer to this should be that she asks no English alms, and she scorns charity which is offered her in lieu of the justice which is her right and her demand. Let landlordism be removed from our country and labour be allowed the wealth which it creates instead of being given to legalised idlers, and no more famine will darken our land or hold Ireland up to the gaze of the civilised world as a nation of paupers. England deprives us annually of some seven millions of money for Imperial taxation, and she allows an infamous land system to rob our country of fifteen or twenty millions more each year to support some nine or twelve thousand lazy landlords, and then, when famine extends its destroying wings over the land, and the dread spectre of death stands sentinel at our thresholds, an appeal to English charity - a begging-box outside the London Mansion House - is paraded before the world, and expected to atone for every wrong inflicted upon Ireland by a heartless and hated Government, and to blot out the records of the most monstrous land code that ever cursed a country or robbed humanity of its birth-right. The press of England may bring whatever charges its prejudices can prompt against this land movement, the Duchess of Marlborough may hurl her gracious wrath at the heads of "heartless agitators," but neither the venomed scurrility of Government organs nor the jealous tirades of politico-prompted charity can rob the much-abused land movement of the credit attached to the following acts. The cry of distress and national danger was first raised by the agitators, and all subsequent action, Government, Viceregal, landlord, and mansion House, to alleviate that distress, was precipitated by the action of the "heartless agitators." The destroying hand of rackrenting and eviction was stricken down for the moment by the influence of the agitation, and the farmers of Ireland were spared some two or three millions with which to meet the distress now looming on

Agrarian calamity threatened Mayo in 1879. After hearing in Claremorris of the plight of the Irishtown tenants, Davitt got local Fenians to organise the meeting on April 20, 1897 which was to be an important step on the road to Westport (June 8) where Parnell advised tenants to 'hold a firm grip on your homesteads and lands'. This led in turn to the founding of the Land League of Mayo (August 16) and to the Irish National Land League, with Parnell as president on October 21. This was the New Departure made flesh.

Right: *Land League Meeting at the Mall, Castlebar, c. 1880* (*Wynne collection*)

their families and country, while the rooftrees of thousands of homesteads were protected from the crowbar brigade; and the civilised world has been appealed to against the existence of a land monopoly which is responsible for a pauperised country, a starved and discontented population, and every social evil now afflicting a patient and industrious people, until a consensus of home and foreign opinion has been evoked in favour of a lasting and efficacious remedy. With these services rendered to Ireland, with a resolve to do the utmost possible to save our people from the danger immediately threatening them, the "heartless agitators" will not relax a single effort or swerve one iota from their original purposes — to haul down the ensign of land monopoly and plant the banner of the "land for the people" upon the dismantled battlements of Irish landlordism.

Michael Davitt, "The crimes of Irish landlordism", from *Irish Bits* (August 13, 1898)

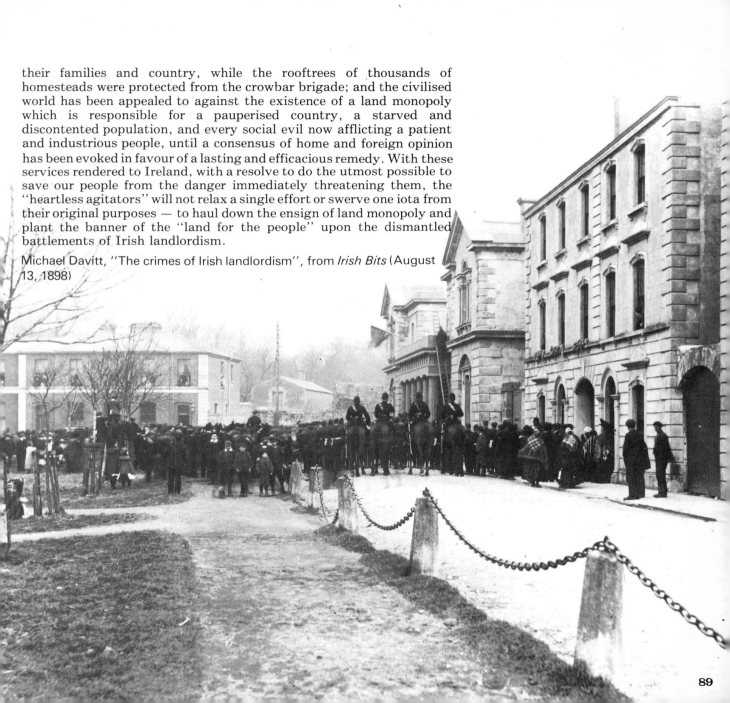

WE SOON SAW that the Republican Army was not going to do anything so desperate as attack. The men were gathering on the parade-ground for the much more agreeable purpose of listening to a speech. A motor-car drove up from the direction of Athlone, entered the camp by the east gate, and rolled across the grass to the parade-ground. There it stopped, and the orator, who was to provide the morning's entertainment, stood up on a seat. I noticed with some surprise that it was a woman.

The ancient Romans, according to Livy, always had speeches before battle, always long, always delivered in the most polished phrases. The Greeks — my recollections of Thucydides are a little vague — but I think the Greeks did the same thing. These classical orators were always generals, a fact which suggests that the course of study in the Staff Colleges of those days must have included elocution. Cromwell's Puritan soldiers liked sermons before and after battle, but the preachers were learned and more or less ordained clergymen, though very long-winded. The Irish system of listening to exhortations from women was new to me, and I felt interested in it. Genevieve and I passed the guardhouse, and made our way towards the parade-ground.

The speaker's back was turned to us and we could not hear what she was saying, but when we were within about fifty yards of her Genevieve suddenly clutched my arm.

"Aunt Josephine!" she said in a tense whisper.

Josephine — well named the Eloquent — was speaking with great force. I could see that she was waving her arms and flinging herself about in a way that imperilled her position on the seat of the car. We approached cautiously and were soon able to hear little bits of what she said, scraps of sentences which she shouted with particular emphasis. "Traitors to the memory of the dead" was a phrase which I heard three times in the course of ten minutes, and each time it sent a thrill down my spine. "The honour of Ireland," proclaimed with emotion which was unmistakably genuine, set my heart beating at far beyond its usual pace. Some one or other, I did not hear his name, had "sold the honour of Ireland." And

Josephine asked with austere dignity what profit man or nation could expect to find in gaining a whole world and losing its immortal soul. Her training as a Sunday-school teacher under Canon Sylvestre had not been entirely wasted. She still remembered several texts of Scripture. An unfortunate class of people whom she first described as "Lackeys of the English Crown," and later on as "Citizens of the

British Empire," were treated with ferocious derision.

"I wonder how long she'll go on," I whispered.

"Hours and hours and hours," said Genevieve. "She always does."

"Well," I replied, "we needn't stay for the whole of it. That's the advantage of not being in the front row. We can slip away whenever we like."

George A Birmingham, *Found Money*, (London, 1923)

GEORGE A BIRMINGHAM was the pen-name of Canon James Owen Hannay. He was born in Belfast in 1865 but served as rector in Westport, Co. Mayo from 1892 to 1913. Regarded as ascendancy by nationalist Ireland he had little sympathy with either the Anglo-Irish revival or the Gaelic League but wrote rather, as did Somerville and Ross, of an Ireland which is an acceptable personal construct. He died in 1950.
Free State Troops in Grattan Street, Sligo (Independent Newspapers)

Eviction Scene, Woodford (*Lawrence Collection, National Library of Ireland*)

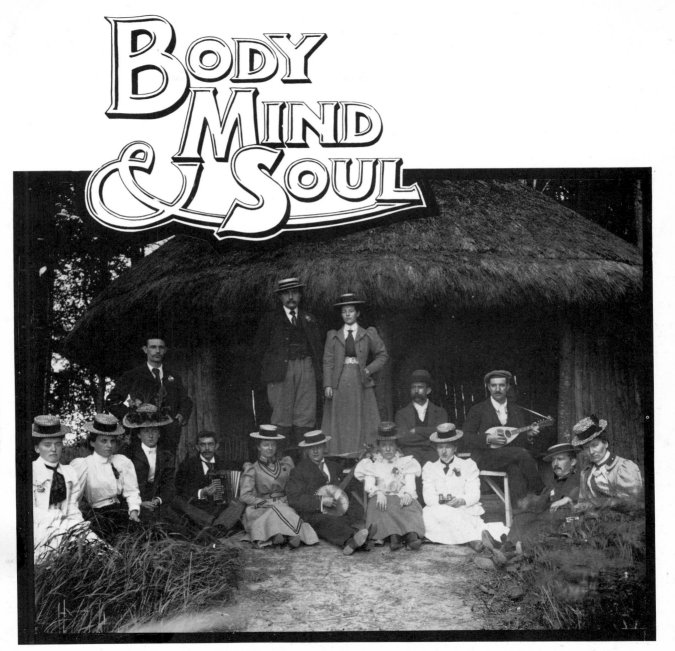

BODY MIND & SOUL

Amateur concert party about 1895, Roscommon Town. (Gavin Collection, Roscommon)

Steve: Is that so? Yellow hair. (*Puts his hand uncertainly to his head.*)

Michelin: You wouldn't be tired listening to her telling out about him. As straight as in the line army! A true fowler with his gun! He never saw the snipe rising, but he'd knock it.

Julia: Stop your talk!

Michelin: The way she has him pictured out you'd say him to be the son of a King, by a Queen.

Steve: Where at all did she meet with such a one?

Julia: Stop your humbugging talk Michelin; You're entirely too supple with the tongue.

Michelin: And the riches he made out in England! There isn't hardly figures enough to count them in arithmetic.

Steve: I never heard of such a one at all.

Michelin: Steve, I believe, is the name he had. Steve Roland.

Steve: Roland! And she made him out so wealthy?

Michelin: A room full of gold in his house. Two labourers stripped of their clothes turning it over with forks.

Steve: She said him to have gold and means?

Michelin: She could have had square diamonds on her hands, and a lady's way of life. Starvation and misery with myself she chose, and he having full bags of coin.

Julia: You have too much chat!

Michelin: Let you go sing again, Julia. Draw down on them some of the old troubles of Ireland, that might make them turn to the cards or the dice.

(*Julia goes to the side again and looks through her sheaf of ballads.*)

Steve (*to Michelin*): Rich she said. To have gold she said? Well, she to have said so, it is so. I didn't tell you that I am a rich man myself!

(*He takes out his little bag, as Julia prepares to sing.*)

Michelin: Come on, so sir, take a turn at the board! (*Calls out.*) Sing out strong, Julia, we have the half of the day wasted! . . . Nominate your colour, sir, while the ball is rolling! Thank you, sir, and the black wins again. The lucky black—one down, two down, any more or any other! Off she goes again! (*They go on playing while Julia sings at the side with her back to them*).

Lady Gregory, *On the Racecourse* (London, 1926) pp.18-21.

LADY GREGORY, born Augusta Persse at Roxborough, Co Galway, 1859 is the mother-figure of the Irish Literary Revival. When her elderly husband Sir William Gregory died in 1892 she turned to writing and to a renewed interest in Irish (which had earned her the nickname of 'the little Fenian' in Gort). A wet day, the presence of Martyn and Yeats and a comfortable room at Dooras House all played their part in the generation of the Irish Literary Theatre. She contributed practically, artistically and politically and has only recently been given her due. *On the Racecourse* is a late reworking of the themes of benevolent deception that she used in *The Jackdaw* and *Twenty-five*. She died in 1932.

Bookies and touts at Castlebar Racetrack, c. 1900. (Wynne Collection)

NO MORE O' YER GOLFIN' FOR ME

Through life I have played all the games that one can,
At football I played on the good Gaelic plan,
You *may* miss the ball but you *must* kick the man,
Or else it won't count to your score.
At Cricket they never knew what I'd be at,
My very first welt laid the bowler out flat,
As they hadn't another I carried me bat,
While they carried him home on a door.

> Golf! Golf! Carry me off!
> Bury me down by the sea.
> The putters may put, still I won't stir a fut,
> No more of yer golfin' for me.

I'm an old fashioned dog to be larnin' new tricks,
But Murphy came round wid two bags full o' sticks,
At Hockey you've one club, but here you have six,
And that's a remarkable thing.
Then Murphy drove off the wee ball. Oh! Begor!
It rose through the air, till it looked like a star,
The head of my driver'd have gone just as far,
If it hadn't been tied with a string.

> Golf! Golf! Carry me off!
> Bury me down by the sea.
> The drivers may drive, but dead or alive,
> No more o' yer golfin' for me.

When I got to the bunker, of clubs I'd just two,
But one was a brass wan, sez I, "That'll do,
If the ball won't go over, I'll make it go through,"
So I slash'd and I hammer'd away.
Then Murphy came up, and sez he, "Ain't it grand,"
Says I, "It's a game I don't quite understand,
How much do they give here for shovellin' sand?
I'd like to get on by the day."

> Golf! Golf! Carry me off!
> Bury me down by the sea.
> The lofters may loft,
> Still my sleep shall be soft,
> No more o' yer golfin' for me.

Percy French, (1906)

(WILLIAM) PERCY FRENCH was born in Clooneyquin, Co Roscommon in 1854. He was educated among other places at Foyle College and graduated from Trinity with a BA in 1876 and B Eng 1881. Described in 1912 by D J O'Donoghue as a 'librettist and song writer of the present day. Before becoming an author he was a civil engineer. The change from drains to strains made him the most famous comic song-writer in English ever and this includes W S Gilbert. He was also a skilled instrumentalist and painter. Known as the author of the 'traditional' American student song, 'Abdulla Bulbul Ameer'. Died 1920.

Castlebar tennis party (*Wynne Collection*)

Lawn Tennis became very popular in Ireland quite soon after the setting of the rules by the All England Club at Wimbledon. Dublin had the distinction of holding the first ever women's championship event in 1879. The earliest courts were hour-glass shaped but rectangular courts soon became standard. The rackets in the picture are at a kind of half-way stage in the evolution of the pre-1880 pear-shaped variety to the modern oval.

IN TENNIS COSTUME

Near the netting which encloses
　　A delightful tennis-space,
Stands Miss Dollie, with the roses
　　Blushing on her pretty face.
Come with me and I will show her
　　To you as she lingers there;
You will really long to know her,
　　She's so sweet and debonair!

Most reluctantly my pen is
　　Forced to mention what is true:
Dolly doesn't play good tennis,
　　And the points she wins are few.
But she's only just beginning—
　　She'll do better, I've no doubt;
And, instead of points, she's winning
　　Love from everyone about.

Watch the fellow in the blazer:
　　Though he knows her play is tame,
Just to please her he will praise her,
　　And lose nearly every game.
Yes, he dearly loves to flatter,
　　Though 'tis plain she cannot play—
But to him this doesn't matter,
　　Since she's won his heart away!

He would fain misunderstand her
　　When she calls out "Thirty love!"
But she'd pose as reprimander
　　If such things he murmured of!
That he fell in love, no wonder.
　　When he felt those eyes of blue.
Can you tell me what in thunder
　　Else a fellow has to do?

For so far is Mistress Dollie,
　　As she stands beside the net,
That 'twould be the greatest folly
　　To attempt her picture—yet
It is safe to say a sweeter
　　Maiden seldom meets the glance;
Would you have the heart to beat her
　　If you ever got the chance?

Anonymous, *In Tennis Costume* (Sligo Independent, 22 September, 1888)

Mo shlán-sa dhuit, a Mhuruisg, a bhí siamsamhail suairc,
Is dho na sléibhtibh breága mealadh bhi ar an taobh deas de'n Chruaich
Ba bhinne liom an roilleach is í 'siubhal suas ó'n tuinn
Ná ceólta na cruinne is bídís uilig cruinn.

Is nuair a eirighim féin ar maidin is feichim i bhfad uaim siar an Chruach
Bíonn mo cnroidhe istigh ar mire is m'aigneadh go buan;
Níl na daoine seo mar chleacht mise síodamhail ná suairc,
Acht mar déanfaidhe de'n ghlas-dair geárrtha amach le tuaigh.

Da bhféadainn-se féin seasamh go labhruigheadh an chuach
D'fhillfinn a bhaile is dhéanfainn mo chuairt.
Meireach an umhluigheacht a bhí agam ariamh do'n ord,
Ni thréigfinn choidhche Muruisg ná aoibhneas na gcuan.

MURUISG is a traditional song in praise of Murrisk, the village from which the ascent of Croagh Patrick is made each summer. (The 'Cruach' of the poem is of course the 'Reek' itself.)

Because of the language decline traditional singing had become much rarer than traditional instrumental music. The effort to keep it alive was made more difficult because the great collectors like Bunting and O'Neill were only interested in the music and many had not the competence to record the words. The new interest in the language inspired by the Gaelic League led to an eleventh hour attempt to rescue the vocal music tradition.

MICHEÁL AND TOMÁS O MÁILLE were born in Connemara in 1880 and 1883. The elder was a schoolteacher and journalist, a frequent contributor to *An Claidheamh Soluis*, the Gaelic League journal. He died in 1911. The younger brother became Professor of Irish at Galway University in 1909. *Amhráin Chlainne Gaedheal* was a collection of Connacht folksongs.

Irish piper (Lawrence Collection, National Library of Ireland)

Left: Scenes during the building and stormy collapse of
Castlebar Catholic Church, 1900 (*Wynne Collection*)

Below: Presbyterian Church, Leenane (*Lawrence
Collection National Library of Ireland*)

"I WAS JUST GOING, ELIZA. If I'd known that Oliver wanted to speak privately to you, I'd have gone sooner."

"No, no, I assure you, Mary."

Mary held out her hand to her brother, saying:

"I suppose I shall not see you again, unless, perhaps, you're stopping the night with Father Higgins. It would be nice if you could do that. You could say Mass for us in the morning."

Father Oliver shook his head.

"I'm afraid I must get back to-night."

"Well, then, good-bye." And Mary went out of the room regretfully, like one who knows that the moment her back is turned all her faults will become the subject of conversation.

"I hear from Mary that some French nuns are coming over, and want to open a school. I hope that won't interfere with yours, Eliza; you spent a great deal of money upon the new wing."

"It will interfere very much indeed; but I'm trying to get some of the nuns to come here, and I hope the Bishop will not permit a new foundation. It's very hard upon us Irish women if we are to be eaten out of house and home by pious foreigners. I'm in correspondence with the Bishop about it. As for Mary —"

"You surely don't think she's going to leave?"

"No, I don't suppose she'll leave; it would be easier for me if she did, but it would give rise to any amount of talk. And where would she go if she did leave, unless she lived with you?"

"My house is too small; besides, she didn't speak of leaving, only that she hadn't yet taken her final vows. I explained that no one will distinguish between the black veil and final vows. Am I not right?"

I think those vows will take a great weight off your mind Oliver. I wish I could say as much for myself."

The Reverend Mother opened a glass door, and brother and sister stood for some time admiring the flower vases that lined the terrace.

"I can't get her to water the geraniums."

"If you'll tell me where I can get a can—"

"You'll excuse me, Reverend Mother."

It was the Sister in charge of the laundry, and,

seeing her crippled arm, Father Oliver remembered that her dress had become entangled in the machinery. He didn't know, however, that the fault lay with Mary, who was told off to watch the machinery and to stop it instantly in case of necessity.

"She can't keep her attention fixed on anything, not even on her prayers, and what she calls piety I should call idleness. It's terrible to have to do with stupid women, and the convent is so full of them that

Rev. Mother Arsenius, (Foxford Collection)

I wonder what is the good of having a convent at all."

"But, Eliza, you don't regret —"

"No, of course I don't regret. I should do just the same again. But don't let us waste our time talking about vocations. I hear enough of that here. I want you to tell me about the music-mistress; that's what interests me."

George Moore, *The Lake* (London, 1905) pp.64, 65 (1914 edition)

The Convent of the Divine Providence was established in Foxford by the Rev. Mother Arsenius (nee Agnes Morrogh-Bernard) in 1891. The district was extremely poor and a year after her school had been set-up she brought the first industry to a very congested district. In 1892, with expert help from J C Smith of Caledon and a grant from the Congested Districts Board and the blessing of Horace Plunkett's Co-operative movement, Providence Woollen Mills were born.

Teaser at work. (Foxford Collection)

"Won't you sit down, Father MacTurnan?" he said casually. "You've been writing to Rome, I see, advocating the revocation of the decree of celibacy. There's no doubt the emigration of Catholics is a very serious question. So far you have got the sympathy of Rome, and I may say of myself; but am I to understand that it was your fear of the religious safety of Ireland that prompted you to write this letter?"

"What other reason could there be?"

Nothing was said for a long while, and then the Bishop's meaning began to break in on his mind; his face flushed, and he grew confused.

"I hope your grace doesn't think for a moment that—"

"I only want to know if there is anyone — if your thoughts ever said, 'Well, if the decree were revoked —'"

"No, your Grace, no. Celibacy has been no burden to me — far from it. Sometimes I feared that it was celibacy that attracted me to the priesthood. Celibacy was a gratification rather than a sacrifice."

"I am glad," said the Bishop, and he spoke slowly and emphatically, "that this letter was prompted by such impersonal motives."

"Surely, your Grace, His Holiness didn't suspect —.."

The Bishop murmured an euphonious Italian name, and Father MacTurnan understood that he was speaking of one of the Pope's secretaries.

"More than once," said Father MacTurnan, "I feared if the decree were revoked, I shouldn't have had sufficient courage to comply with it."

And then he told the Bishop how he had met Norah Flynn on the road. An amused expression stole into the Bishop's face, and his voice changed.

"I presume you do not contemplate making marriage obligatory; you do not contemplate the suspension of the facilities of those who do not take wives?"

"It seems to me that exception should be made in favour of those in Orders, and of course in favour of those who have reached a certain age like your Grace."

The Bishop coughed, and pretended to look for some

Pilgrims at Knock 1892 (Wynne Collection, Castlebar)

Left: *Corpus Christi Procession, Ballina (Lawrence Collection, The National Library of Ireland.)*

paper which he had mislaid.

This was one of the many points that I discussed with Father Michael Meehan.''

"Oh, so you consulted Father Meehan," the Bishop said, looking up.

"He came in the day I was reading over my Latin translation before posting it. I'm afraid the ideas that I submitted to the consideration of His Holiness have been degraded by my very poor Latin. I should have wished Father Meehan to overlook my Latin, but he refused. He begged of me not to send the letter.''

"Father Meehan," said his Grace, "is a great friend of yours. Yet nothing he could say could shake your resolution to write to Rome?"

"Nothing," said Father MacTurnan. "The call I received was too distinct and too clear for me to hesitate.''

"Tell me about this call."

Father MacTurnan told the Bishop that the poor man had come out of the workhouse because he wanted to be married, and that Mike Mulhare would not give him his daughter until he had earned the price of a pig. "And as I was talking to him I heard my conscience say, 'No one can afford to marry in Ireland but the clergy.' We all live better than our parishioners.''

George Moore, *The Untilled Field*, (Dublin, 1902) pp. 114-115.

". . . I BEHELD ALL AT ONCE, standing out from the gable, and rather to the west of it, three figures which, on more attentive inspection, appeared to be that of the Blessed Virgin, St Joseph, and St John. That of the Blessed Virgin was life-size, the others apparently either not so big or not so high as her figure, they stood out a little distance from the gable wall, and, as well as I could judge, a foot and a half or two feet from the ground. The Virgin stood erect, with eyes raised to heaven, her hands elevated to the shoulders or a little higher, the palms inclined slightly towards the shoulders or the bosom; she wore a large cloak of a white colour, hanging in full folds and somewhat loosely around her shoulders, and fastened to the neck; she wore a crown on the head, rather a large crown, and it appeared to me somewhat yellower than the dress or robes worn by Our Blessed Lady. . ."

Testimony of Mary Beirne concerning the events of Thursday, August 21, 1879 at Knock, Co. Mayo.

"'THE HEDGE SCHOOLMASTER was not the sort of man whom Carleton and Lever have lampooned, no such thing; he was generally a well-informed stranger, the scion perhaps of some noble family who had been disinherited by Elizabeth, or by James the First, or by the inhuman Cromwell. The school boys carried with them to these masters Homer's *Iliad* and *Odyssey*, *Paradise Lost* and *Paradise Regained*, the *History of Greece and Rome*, the *Arabian Nights*, Thomas-a-Kempis, Dr. Gallagher and Keating, the *Old Testament*, Sallust in English, Ovid, Ward's *Cantos*, McGeoghegan's *History of Ireland*, and a hundred and one other books. Where they all came from is one of the things that now astonishes me, for these books were in every peasant's cottage on the little loft over the fireplace, along with the wool-cards, the balls of yarn, and the spindles; there the books rested, some without covers, and all of them stained with smoke. When a boy had his *Odyssey* read, he exchanged it with another chap for his *Iliad*, and so on. They spent seven or eight years at this kind of work, and got them off by heart, as we called it.

"'Each boy and girl had a favourite Grecian or Roman hero; some admired Socrates, some Leonidas, some Lycurgus, some Xenophon, and some Cincinnatus. The girls were taught to admire Susanna, Judith, the mother of the Machabees, Lucretia, and Virginia, while we all admired

Scholars at Roscommon, c.1890, photographed by R W Simmons of Galway (Gavin Collection).

Hannibal. Often we had refined boxing matches, with each boy standing up for his favourite hero. This business was conducted according to the rules of the ring, for we had two seconds and a timekeeper, whose business it was to see that one boy didn't hit the other below the belt, or when he was down.

"'The children were also taught how to sit at table, and how to handle a knife and fork. They were taught to salute and respect the aged, and to bow and draw their bob or forelock to all strangers; anyhow, the bob got its own share of pulling, for, alas, we had no cap to raise. When these ragged little boys, some wearing trousers, some wearing flannel petticoats, or dresses like females, left off going to school and began to handle their spades, their minds were made. In fact, they had the minds of fully-grown, noble men and women, for, to their credit, let it be said that some of the girls were the cleverest in the schools.

"'These little boys and girls when they left school were better informed than the fully grown men of the present day. One of them knew more about the world than all the National School boys in the parish if they were all melted down and cast into one huge National School boy of this day. It was in these hedge schools that the Irish peasantry learned to be steadfast, honourable and truthful, and to have fortitude, so that when the penal laws and the persecution set in, they thought of the woman and her seven sons in the Bible, of Daniel in the lion's den, and the fiery furnace, and they held to the faith of their fathers like grim death, and won. I wonder, if the penal laws and the persecution set in now in this frivolous age with its threepenny novels, novelettes, and penny horror tales, would we be able to give such a good account of ourselves. Indeed, I fear not.'"

James Berry; *Tales of the West of Ireland* (Dublin 1966)

JAMES BERRY was born at Bunowen near Louisburgh, Co. Mayo in 1842. His early education was at a hedge school, but when he moved to Carna, his uncle, a local clergyman, added to this perhaps inadequate beginning. His stories, originally published in the 'Mayo News' (1910-1013), are lively extravagant and implicitly hero-worshipping. The stories were edited and published in book form as *Tales of the West of Ireland* by Dolmen Press in 1966 and edited by Gertrude M Horgan. He died in 1914.

The National School system was established in 1831 in spite of known objections by the churches. The schools were intended to be multidenominational with a common curriculum of the three 'R's, geography, grammar, and book-keeping and needlework for girls. By 1861 they had become in fact denominational schools with clerical managers. School began at 9.30 and ended at 3 pm in winter and 5 pm in summer. Teachers were forbidden to live above licensed premises, could not take part in politics, were subservient to the managers and badly paid.

INDEX OF AUTHORS

Street Front, Castlebar, showing the extent of photographer Wynne's business interests as newsagent, auctioneer and furniture salesman (Wynne Collection)

Harbour, Clare Island (*Lawrence Collection, National Library of Ireland*)

Acknowledgements

*Honeymoon Couple 1912 (Lynch
Collection Lisdoonvarna)*

For kind permission to reprint copyright material, the following acknowledgements are made:- For a poem by William Butler Yeats to M. B. Yeats, Miss Anne Yeats and The Macmillan Company of London and Basingstoke; for an extract from George Moore to J. C. Medley and R. G. Medley; for an extract from George Moore to Colin Smythe Limited, Publishers; for an extract from Lady Gregory to the Lady Gregory Estate and Colin Smythe Limited, Publishers; for an extract from Douglas Hyde to the Dr. Douglas Hyde Trust; for a poem from "Amhráin Chlainne Gaedheal" to Conradh na Gaeilge; for an extract from Somerville and Ross to Sir Patrick Coghill and Chatto and Windus; for an extract from Líam O'Flaherty to the author and Jonathan Cape Ltd.; for an extract from Padraic Ó Conaire to Sáirséal agus Dill; for an extract from Grace Rhys to the author and J. M. Dent and Sons Ltd.; for an extract from James Berry to the Dolmen Press; for extracts from M. McDonnell Bodkin and Joseph Guinan to Gill and MacMillan Ltd.

For kind permission to use photographs the following acknowledgements are made:- For photographs from the Lawrence Collection to the director of the National Library of Ireland; to Mr. Desmond Wynne of Castlebar; to Liam Jordan of Ballinasloe; to Rev. Mother M. Enda of Foxford; to the director of the State Paper Office, Dublin; to Mrs. L. Stephens and Trinity College Library; to Miss Gavin of Roscommon.

FACES OF THE PAST

BY BRIAN MERCER WALKER

ULSTER LIFE 1880~1915